BEYOND BELIEF

BEYOND BELIEF
Psychotherapy and Religion

edited by
Samuel M. Stein

David M. Black   Patrick Casement

David H. Clark   Murray Cox

Patrick Gallwey   Robert D. Hinshelwood

Judith Hubback   Judith Issroff

Moisés Lemlij   Eduardo Montagne

Colin Murray Parkes   Janet Sayers

Neville Symington

London
KARNAC BOOKS

First published in 1999 by
H. Karnac (Books) Ltd.
58 Gloucester Road
London SW7 4QY

British Library Cataloguing in Publication Data

A C.I.P for this book is available from the British Library

ISBN 1 85575 186 0

10 9 8 7 6 5 4 3 2 1

Edited, designed, and produced by Communication Crafts

Printed in Great Britain by Polestar Wheatons Ltd, Exeter

For
Jenny,
a fellow traveller

CONTENTS

vii

CONTRIBUTORS

David M. Black was born in South Africa in 1941. Educated in Africa and Scotland, he took a First-Class degree in Philosophy at Edinburgh and an M.A. in Eastern Religions under Ninian Smart at Lancaster. Since 1974, he has been on the staff of the Westminster Pastoral Foundation. He is a Founder Member of the Institute of Psychotherapy and Counselling. David Black trained as a psychoanalyst with the British Psycho-Analytical Society and now works mainly in private practice in London. He is especially interested in the implications of psychoanalysis for a wider understanding of the nature of science and values.

Patrick Casement was born in Surrey in 1935. He was educated at Winchester College before going to Cambridge, where he read Anthropology and Theology. He worked for ten years as a social worker, in the Probation Service, and in the Family Welfare Association. Patrick Casement is now in full-time practice as a psychoanalyst, having trained first with the British Association of Psychotherapists and then with the Institute of Psycho-Analysis in London. He is now a training and supervising analyst for the

British Psycho-Analytical Society. He regards himself as a reverently questioning agnostic, respecting religion and religious experience as a part of life.

David H. Clark was born and grew up in Edinburgh. He obtained his B.A. degree in 1941 before qualifying as a medical doctor in 1943. After serving in the armed forces he trained as a psychiatrist, becoming a Fellow of both the Royal College of Physicians and the Royal College of Psychiatrists. This was followed in 1972 by a Ph.D. Dr Clark practised as a consultant psychiatrist at Fulbourn Hospital in Cambridge, serving as the Administrator of the hospital for over thirty years. He was a member of the Cambridge Humanists, an Honorary Member of the Institute of Group Analysis, and an Associate Lecturer in Psychiatry at the University of Cambridge. He also served as Vice-Chairman of MIND and as a consultant for the World Health Organisation. Dr. Clark has written two books: *Administrative Therapy* and *Social Therapy in Psychiatry*. His interests lie in Eastern religion and individual spirituality.

Murray Cox was born in Birmingham in 1931. He was educated at Kingswood School in Bath before entering Cambridge. He completed his medical training in London, and later he specialized in psychiatry and psychotherapy. Dr Cox was a Fellow of the Royal College of Psychiatrists and practised as a Consultant Psychotherapist at Broadmoor Hospital for twenty-five years. He had a special interest in Shakespeare studies and was an Honorary Research Fellow of the Shakespeare Institute, University of Birmingham. He was also an Honorary Member of the Institute of Group Analysis. Dr. Cox's interest in human nature included forensic psychotherapy, mutative metaphors and aesthetic imperatives. He had an intermittent affiliation with the Christian Existentialists and felt that religion was an integral part of everything. Sadly, Murray Cox died in 1997.

Patrick Gallwey was born in Surrey in 1929. He was educated at St. Margaret's School in Devon and Dauntseys School in Wiltshire before undertaking his medical training at St. Thomas' Hospital Medical School in London. Dr Gallwey completed the higher professional training in psychiatry and is a Fellow of the Royal College of Psychiatrists. He works part-time as a consultant forensic psychiatrist in the NHS and is also a visiting psychiatrist at HMP Exeter. Dr. Gallwey trained as a psychoanalyst through the Institute of Psychoanalysis, and has a private analytic practice as well as a medico-legal consultancy. He has no religious affiliation. His interest in human nature and religion relates to the understanding of the roots of sanity and goodness, and the link between imagination and reason.

Robert D. Hinshelwood was born in London in 1938, and he trained at UCH Medical School, deciding from early on to specialize in psychiatry. In the 1960s and 1970s, he became involved in the therapeutic community movement and anti-psychiatry, and he eventually trained at the Institute of Psycho-Analysis. For many years, Dr Hinshelwood ran a local department of psychotherapy in west London. More latterly he returned to therapeutic communities, when he became Clinical Director of the Cassel Hospital, and has just recently taken up post as Professor of Psychoanalysis at the Centre for Psychoanalytic Studies at the University of Essex. His published works include many on the psychodynamic understanding of organizations, as well as two books on Kleinian psychoanalysis and a recent addition on psychoanalysis and ethics called *Therapy or Coercion? Does Psychoanalysis Differ from Brainwashing*.

Judith Hubback was born in London in 1917 and was christened into the Church of England. She first attended school in Paris and later at Downe House, a girl's boarding-school in Newbury. Mrs Hubback then went up to Cambridge where she took a First Class degree in History. She trained as an analytical psychologist through the Society of Analytical Psychology in London and continues to practise privately. In addition to writing learned articles, poetry and a novel, she edited the *Journal of Analytical Psychology* for many years as well as the Library of Analytical Psychology. Judith Hubback has wide-ranging interests in history, literature, international politics, public affairs and family life. Her interest in religion revolves around its historical background, an academic perspective and her own personal experience.

Judith Issroff is South African-born, British and Israeli. She completed her medical studies at the University of Witwatersrand, Johannesburg. As a Consultant in the Tavistock Clinic Adolescent Unit she became a Founder Member of the Royal College of Psychiatrists and ran training groups for senior prison personnel from 1971 to 1977. She qualified to work psychoanalytically with adults, adolescents and children through the British Psycho-Analytical Society, is a Member of the Group Analytic Society and is registered in the Conflict Resolution International roster. She drafted recommendations to encourage mental health professionals to promote non-violent conflict containment and resolution, and she co-founded the Israeli Association for Social Care, Health, and Solution of Conflicts which aims to implement such recommendations. She is active in the International Association of University Women and in the Jerusalem Council for Children and Youth and has been funded by UNICEF to consult with psychosocial rehabilitation projects in Mozambique. Her wide-ranging interests include Holocaust studies, trauma, refugees, painting, science, literature, forestry, comparative religion, ethics, and philosophy. Judith Issroff has written about a broad range of topics, and her poetry has been published in several countries.

Moisés Lemlij was born in Peru in 1938. He was educated at the University of San Marcos in Lima and at the University of London. After completing his medical training, he took his Doctorate in medicine in Peru and a diploma in psychological medicine in England. He is a member of the Royal College of Psychiatrists and trained though the British Psycho-Analytical Society. In Peru, besides his private practice and institutional commitments, one of his interests has been to apply psychoanalytic concepts to social, historical and anthropological issues. In relation to religion, he has edited *Al final del Camino* [At the End of the Road] and *En el Nombre del Señor* [In the Name of the Lord].

Eduardo Montagne was born in Lima, Peru, in 1946. He was educated by the Jesuits in Lima. Completing his studies, he entered the Order and studied Philosophy (Madrid) and Theology (Mexico and Rome). He trained as a psychotherapist at the Peruvian Psychoanalytical Psicotherapy Institute, completing his training in psychoanalysis later on. Retired from the Jesuits' Order, he is presently an Associate Member of the Peruvian Psychoanalytic Society and practises his clinical work privately. His studies and previous experience stimulated his interest in the theme of motivation and religious ideas, and in the problem of defining normality and pathology. At present he is Professor of Psychopathology at the Psychoanalytical Psychotherapy School in Lima, and he has published several psychoanalytic papers.

Colin Murray Parkes was born in London in 1928. He was educated at Epsom College and London University. After completing his medical training, he specialized as a psychiatrist and is a Fellow of the Royal College of Psychiatrists. He practises as a Consultant Psychiatrist at St. Christopher's Hospital in Sydenham and at St. Joseph's Hospice in Hackney. Dr. Parkes has no religious affiliation. His interest in human behaviour relates to the provision of care, research and teaching in regard to terminal care and bereavement. He is currently editing a book entitled *Cross-Cultural Aspects of Death and Bereavement*. Dr. Parkes regards spiritual care as an important aspect of the work of doctors, particularly those who work with the dying and the bereaved.

Janet Sayers was born in London in 1945. She first learned about psychoanalysis at Darlington Hall School, before studying Philosophy and Psychology at Cambridge. Ms. Sayers then trained as a Clinical Psychologist at the Tavistock Clinic in London and became involved in the women's movement on moving to Canterbury in 1970. She lectures in Psychology, Social Studies and Women's Studies at the University of Kent and works part-time as a psychotherapist. Her books include *Biological Politics*, *Sexual Contradictions*, and *Mothering Psychoanalysis*. She is currently working on a collection of feminist psychoanalytic work tales.

Samuel M. Stein was born and brought up in Johannesburg, South Africa. After graduating from the University of the Witwatersrand Medical School in 1986, he completed his internship at Baragwanath Hospital in Soweto. In 1988, he moved to the United Kingdom to undertake his registrar training in general psychiatry in Oxford. Dr Stein graduated with a B.A. in Psychology and Criminology before completing his higher training in Child and Adolescent Psychiatry at St. Mary's Hospital in London. A Member of the Royal College of Psychiatrists, he is currently working as a Consultant in Child, Adolescent, and Family Psychiatry in South Bedfordshire. Samuel Stein has maintained a long-standing interest in psychoanalysis and psychotherapy and has written a number of articles within these fields. He is co-author of two books: *Essentials of Psychotherapy* and *Psychotherapy in Practice: A Life in the Mind.*

Neville Symington is a psychoanalyst in private practice in Sydney, Australia. He trained at the Institute of Psycho-Analysis in London and prior to that had qualifications in Philosophy, Theology and Psychology. He held a senior staff position in the Adult Department of the Tavistock Clinic from 1976 to 1985. Mr Symington was also chairman of the Psychology Discipline for the Adult and Adolescent Departments at the Tavistock. In 1986 he migrated to Sydney, where he was chairman of the Sydney Institute for Psycho-Analysis from 1987 to 1993. He is the author of *The Analytic Experience, Narcissism: A New Theory, Emotion and Spirit,* and *The Making of a Psychotherapist.* Together with his wife Joan, he is joint-author of *The Clinical Thinking of Wilfred Bion.* Neville Symington has lectured widely in Australia and New Zealand, and also in India, the United Kingdom and the United States of America.

Robert D. Hinshelwood

What an interesting idea to set psychotherapists on the trail of the spiritual.

In the 1880s, Frederic Myers and the other researchers of the Society for Psychical Research (commonly known as the SPR) began to look for hard evidence of the spirit world. They chose methods that came directly from the material sciences. At that time, chemistry, physics, and biology had produced amazing technological advances. Communication, industrial production and household gadgetry, railways, steam power, photography, the telegraph, factory machinery, and public health all had created a self-consciously advancing culture that believed that the completion of the project of knowing everything was very near. So the methods of the material sciences must have seemed the obvious choice to employ in the search for spirits, despite the latter being supernatural and immaterial.

Not surprisingly, that approach failed. In fact quite soon afterwards, Hughlings Jackson demonstrated that all the auras, automatisms, and trances of spiritualist mediums were present in temporal lobe epilepsy. In an amazingly ironic twist, which only

true life can bring, Jackson's first and most dramatic case of temporal lobe epilepsy turned out to be Alfred Myers, the brother of
the chief researcher of the SPR.

This suggests that proper investigation by a natural science
method produces a conclusion thoroughly in keeping with its
premises—a material cause. The principle might be that to get
the right kind of results, one needs to start with the right kind
of method. The bright idea behind this book is that a science that
deals with the immaterial might be more apt for finding out
about the immaterial world of God. So psychotherapy, dealing
with the immaterial, at least the immaterial mind, could perhaps
throw light on the immaterial substances of religious beliefs and
experiences.

The burden once put upon natural scientists is here shoul-
dered by psychotherapists. We are invited to ask: Can psychotherapy go beyond belief?

This collection of essays is a wonderfully varied set of answers
by a wide range of people—from left-wing socialists to a clutch of
ex-theologians, from psychiatrists to psychoanalysts, Jungians to
Freudians, Jews to Catholics, agnostics to the devout. And how
agreeable such an encompassing group seems to be when it
comes to God. They write, almost without exception, with a serious sympathy, gently negotiated disagreements and reservations,
and an almost hallowed kind of honouring. In short, rather like
entering a cathedral.

It feels uncomfortable to have to risk contributing a discordant
tone. But unfortunately the reverence that is habitually aimed at
religion tends to bring out in me a surge of irreverence. This, I
have to acknowledge, must come from my own contrary character. Religion always brings to my mind those sepia photographs
of mission stations with posed natives in ill-fitting brassieres or
baggy trousers and crumpled felt hats, looking degraded and
helpless. I tend to think of those disasters of war that come out of
ethnicity or moral rectitude caused, or inflamed, by religious belief; and those rituals of humiliation, penance, or torture inflicted
(sometimes self-inflicted) on countless generations of devout human bodies.

But that is merely religion in its institutionalized form. To a
(wo)man the essayists would probably agree with me. They more

or less all repudiate "organized religion". They reject dogma and (mostly) rituals. They revert simply to "natural religion", the deeply personal religious experience of a mystical kind.

That resort to a common denominator is a characteristically contemporary attitude to the diversity of religions. We now call it pluralism. In contrast, when Hellenic culture expanded during the fifth century BC, thoughtful men were confronted with the fact that religion is relative to one's culture. Different places had different gods. This led to a profound scepticism about belief. Socratic enquiry was the outcome, a belief in the question rather than the answer. And enlightened enquiry became the scourge of religion for a thousand years.

When, however, Christianity encountered different cultures and religious beliefs in the course of nineteenth-century colonialism, it had a rather different and Eurocentric response, clinging more tenaciously to "right" answers (Christian ones) than to right questions. And religion became the scourge of enlightened enquiry.

However, by the end of the twentieth century, a curious mixture of right-mindedness with Christian toleration has grown up. Pluralism is a charitable (though possibly condescending) attitude: we may be different, but we share in common the right to believe what we want to.

If there were indeed a true experience that is beyond materialism, what would it be? When sometime in the late 1950s as a student I read Aldous Huxley's *Perennial Philosophy* (1946), I did think that he was pointing to a core experience. I had in some respects a similar reaction to Colin Wilson's *The Outsider* (1956). I was unhappy at medical school, and the notion of the ineffable, the unknown, and the excluded seemed, if not to fill a gap, at least to identify it. These were intimations of a dualism—a belief that the transcendent and incommunicable beyondness existed in a separate domain from my bodily functioning. Though I know that experiences are emergent from the body, I haven't got away from hankering for something more.

David Clark's account of his out-of-body experiences is the gem in this book. This poignant state came to him as he faced the end of his marriage, retirement from his prominent career, and the decline of his health. He takes his new transcendent experiences exactly at face value in his exuberant way. By their nature, these experiences carry a total conviction.

Solitary contemplation of the infinite and the eternal may (or does) create a dizzying mystical vortex. But what is the nature of that experience? And can we ask such a question? These essays in general start by exploring personal experiences—psychotherapists turning their trade upon themselves. In accord with principles, they explore their childhood and do so with an ease to be expected of psychotherapists. It seems, at least for children who later become psychotherapists, that they describe a regime of imposed answers and ritual instructions. It is a backdrop against which the rest of life is a journey—not to enquire but to receive. To enquire therefore leads to revolt. And then, at some point, a formative struggle reaches a new contract with adulthood.

Psychotherapists naturally approach all experiences psychologically. In some ways there is a competition. Religion (in its institutional form) hijacks morality and ethics. It often hijacks mental health too. Psychotherapists are tempted therefore to reclaim therapy—morality, too—as psychological approaches to the person and to personal development. We can probably outdo the church by a very long margin in understanding ordinary experiences. And Pat Gallwey's piece is the most eloquent and forceful in putting this. The religious organization of belief systems is often transparently defensive against the ordinary pain of life—and particularly of death (for example, the reassuring "resurrection principle" described by Patrick Casement). Religion offers itself, too, as an opiate to dull the pain of the masses of people that our society condemns to poverty and neglect—though nowadays this offer is more often taken up by immigrant groups.

Religion often stands shoulder to shoulder with the prejudices of nationalism and ethnicity. It offers community in the midst of loneliness. It appropriates orgasmic states as holy ecstasy. These are psychological truths which stand in contrast to religious claims on mental health and moral virtue. Religious "iconography", as Janet Sayers claims, serves communication, communal solidarity, and personal peace amidst the restless questioning. But "psychologizing" religion is not really fulfilling the project of this book. Can psychotherapists enlighten us about what is beyond psychology? Psychotherapists, like everyone else, may be frustrated, lonely, and frightened by the unknown, but our method confines us to listening to experiences—not to answering questions about the unknown. Psychotherapy remains stubbornly Socratic in prioritizing questions over answers, and therefore promises to be merely ordinary—and unrevealing.

Like natural science in the physical world, psychotherapy is constrained by its own terms. It is restricted to the frame of Kantian space and time. Mystical experience is crucially different. It does not give answers, but, more than that, it does not even ask the questions. Transcendent states work in a different way. They render the Kantian frame no longer pressing at all. Transcendence dissolves enquiry entirely.

It would seem hard to argue that psychotherapy can go beyond its own limits and make comment on the mystical. By transcending itself, it would therefore *be* mystical. To remain psychotherapy it must unfortunately stick to its field, to its terms, and, most unfortunately of all, to its space/time framework. This leaves the unknowable, unenquiring spirit pristinely untouched.

Possibly, therefore, the project that this book represents is as misguided as those of the nineteenth century Society for Psychical Research. Ironically, in the twentieth century we now "research" psychotherapy itself using methods based on the drug trial—and that was invented for the thoroughly material purpose of showing the effects of physical substances on the biological brain. Our latter-day Society for Psychotherapy Research (also an SPR) may be as up-a-gum-tree as its predecessor namesake.

Nevertheless, if you, the readers of these essays, are as enjoyably provoked and frustrated as I have been, this book will amply realize its subsidiary project—to stimulate our ordinary reflections on the unknown.

INTRODUCTION

"Man is what he believes."

Anton Chekhov

Psychoanalysis and psychotherapy differ from many other theoretical paradigms and clinical practices in that the therapist is required to utilize, in a carefully modulated manner, his or her own identity and emotional reactions as the basis for understanding the patient's perspective. Rather than simply being able to engage in psychotherapeutic work at a cognitive or rational level, few individuals who choose to understand human interactions in this way are left unchanged by their personal and professional explorations. However, would-be psychotherapists do not always realize the impact that psychoanalytic study and experience may have on their individual development.

When I first embarked on my own analysis and related academic learning, I found my increasing interest in and commitment to psychoanalytic thinking extremely exciting. But it also required a great deal of change and adaptation in both professional and personal spheres. One of the most complex modifications that I encountered was the way in which my religious beliefs began to change. I found that as my psychoanalytic understanding increased, my religious beliefs decreased. I therefore came to perceive psychoanalysis and religion as antithetical paradigms, and yet I did not want to relinquish either belief: Judaism represented a safe and secure past, whereas psychoanalysis represented an exciting and enlightened future.

Whilst making a circuitous and muddled way through the dilemmas inherent in both the overlap and the conflict between psychotherapy and religion, I read in one of Charles Rycroft's works of a book called *The God I Want* (1967) by James Mitchell. It comprised a series of short essays of the same title by analysts, authors, theologians and others describing their approach to religion and their own personal theology. It was thought-provoking to read of the religious dilemmas faced by other people, as well as of how they had resolved them. However, whilst Rycroft's own contribution (as an analyst) to the book was very helpful, others drawn from fields outside psychoanalysis were less so. An additional problem was that Mitchell's publication was over thirty years old, no longer in print and rarely available.

Stimulated by my own personal experiences, I developed the idea to collate a series of similar and up-to-date essays written by psychiatrists, psychoanalysts and psychotherapists on the interaction between psychotherapy and religion. Perhaps in doing this, I would come to understand how others with an overlapping interest in both psychotherapy and religion had come to decide on a way forward that was personally acceptable and satisfying. As reflected in some of the chapter titles, I originally requested contributors to write on "The God I Want", although this later generalized to "The Spirit of God", based on a poem by Walt Whitman.

All of the contributors have given willingly of their time, their effort and themselves. They agreed to provide the essays free of charge as the royalties generated by the book will be donated to the promotion of training and research within the field of psychotherapy. Each of them seems to have gained something from writing their contribution, and collating these essays and bringing *Beyond Belief* to print has proved a remarkable journey in its own right for me. I can only hope that it encourages similar personal and professional explorations in those who read and enjoy this book.

Samuel M. Stein
Pitchcott, 1999

BEYOND BELIEF

CHAPTER ONE

"The God I want"

David M. Black

"Do not seek to imitate the men of old: seek what they sought."

Zen proverb

Although the phrase has been abused, I believe that it is true that we have reached a "new age" in religious thought. This is not a matter of a movement prepared to believe in divination by crystals, pendulums, ley-lines, or the Great Pyramid. Nor has it anything to do with the "Age of Aquarius". It is to do with the geographical opening up of the world, the huge illumination of the historical past which has taken place in the last 150 years, the encounter on-the-level of the different religious traditions, and the inevitable modification of particular traditions which must follow. It is also, of course, to do with modern attitudes of mind. To us, miracle stories are no longer sources of devout wonder but of scientific scepticism; particular doctrines are no longer simple statements, true or false, of the way divine reality *is*, they are also historical events that have occurred at a particular moment in a continuous, developing history.

It is possible, in dismay at these enormous changes, to retreat from them. Typically retreat takes one of two forms. One is a blind and dogmatic reassertion of traditional teaching with an implicit or explicit rejection of the idea that modern developments have any value at the religious level (if they have importance, it is purely destructive). This path leads to fundamentalism. It has been taken to some extent by the Catholic Church under Pope John Paul II, and also by certain Hindu, Muslim, and Jewish sects. The attraction of the fundamentalist path is easy to understand, and its prevalence (and often violence) should remind us how very frightening it is to have one's fundamental framework of apprehension challenged. These believers have structured the world in accord with certain narratives and aphorisms, and we may imagine that to have these questioned threatens them with the "nameless dread"—the psychotic-like terrors—that modern psychoanalysis attributes to the unheld or uncontained baby (Bion, 1967).

The other retreat is one widely practised by sophisticated Westerners. It is the heir to the late-nineteenth-century belief that religion was just a sort of second-rate science giving an account of the origin and history of the world, and that we now know better. In *The Future of an Illusion* (1927c), Freud put it crisply: religious beliefs were "fairy-tales".

This reaction developed into another sort of fundamentalism. The cult of the measurable fact, entirely appropriate to physical science and its material applications, became a tyranny that mocked the value-creating feelings and intuitions out of which religion springs. Though now on the wane, this scientific fundamentalism is still widespread, particularly in the life-sciences. Eminent biologists such as Richard Dawkins continue to speak with this confident, nineteenth-century voice, whereas those at the forefront of physics—including Einstein, de Broglie, Heisenberg, and others—have been impelled to embrace a wider vision (see Wilber, 1984, for a remarkable anthology of such writings by physicists). I shall call this second retreat, which idealizes the methods and assumptions of positivistic science, "scientism".

To summarize: my view is that we are entering a "new age" of religious thought, made possible by the confluence of different religious and scientific traditions which can now, for the first time, meet with an attitude of mutual respect. So disturbing is this development that we are tempted to retreat from it into an idealization of familiar things: religious people into religious fundamentalism, non-religious people into scientism. My own profession, psychoanalysis, at its inception very much tended to make itself part of the latter movement.

* * *

But, if we risk being open, what do we discover?

Religions and Languages

In the early 1960s, two rival theories about the origins of the universe were current: Hermann Bondi and Fred Hoyle had put forward a theory of continuous creation (the "steady-state" theory); A. G. E. Lemaitre and George Gamow had put forward a theory in which the universe had a very definite starting point (the "big-bang" theory). To the lay-onlooker, it seemed there was little but intuition to choose between them. In 1965, however, a microwave background radiation said to be the "echo of the big bang" was discovered throughout space, and since then more and more evidence has accumulated. The big-bang story is now told with masses of interrelated and convincing detail, and the steady state theory seems cumbersome and non-explanatory.

This accumulated evidence does not make it certain, although certainly more likely, that the big-bang theory is correct. We expect such a pattern in the history of physical science—that increasing evidence will gradually tip the scales in favour of this or that of a pair of rival theories, and it makes good sense to describe this as an "advance" in our knowledge. Thomas Kuhn (1962) has described the development of science as a series of paradigm shifts, but this does not imply that any paradigm is as good as any other. Absolute truth may not be attainable, but a satisfactory new paradigm is one that embraces more facts and has greater depth of explanatory power than its predecessor.

Psychoanalysis too can tell a story of "advance" of this kind. It has shifted from being a drive theory, in which human motivation is above all powered by the need to discharge certain physiological tensions, towards being an object-relations theory in which we seek particular persons with whom to enact certain sorts of relationship. This is clearly progress, because it allows more of the observed detail to be elegantly accounted for. Such fundamental passions as grief, guilt, remorse, envy, and jealousy can fit coherently into this new picture.

It is generally said that such "advances" do not occur in religion. The alternative to fundamentalism is usually taken to be a post-modern pluralism, where any religion is as good as any other and there is no competition between them (such tolerance is sometimes taken aback when it encounters the religion of the Aztecs).

I want to borrow from the theologian Raimon Panikkar a comparison of religions with languages. Different religions, says Panikkar, are like different languages: you can say true things in every language, but there are some true things you can say in one language which you can't say in another; there will also be true things you can say in the second which can't be said in the first (Panikkar, 1981). Anyone who has attempted to do translation, even between close-kindred languages like German and English, will know the force of this comparison.

If we take this comparison as a starting-point, it allows us to say much that is simplifying and illuminating. Languages are not only rich, expressive, and truth-telling; they can also be shoddy, impoverished, or rigid. The richness of Shakespeare cannot be translated into French; the nobility of Homer cannot be translated into modern-day English.

Not surprisingly, contacts between religions have often started off with a great deal of misunderstanding. When the first Christian missionaries arrived in India, they were welcomed with open arms by the swamis, who were delighted to hear of yet another incarnation of Vishnu. Tibetan Buddhists teaching Westerners the *phowa* practice (a visualization technique) will standardly ask them to imagine a figure who for them represents wisdom and compassion—the Buddha, Padmasambhava, Jesus Christ, the Virgin Mary—unhesitatingly putting all these figures in a row: to the Tibetan, they are all equally bodhisattvas.

Similarly, the translation in the other direction, from East to West, is not easy. We no longer, like the first explorers, describe the Buddha as a god; but are we right to say, as is standardly said nowadays, that Buddhism is "atheistic"? Certainly not, if that word has the aggressive quality that it usually has; but even if we confine it to its bare, literal meaning, I doubt if it catches much of the reality.

Here is how a modern Vietnamese Buddhist Master, Thich Nhat Hanh (1995, pp. 150–151), who knows the West well, discusses the topic:

> A good theologian is one who says almost nothing about God, even though the word "theology" means "discourse about God". It is risky to talk about God. The notion of God might be an obstacle for us to touch God as love, wisdom, and mindfulness. The Buddha was very clear about this. He said, "You tell me you are in love with a beautiful woman, but when I ask you, 'What is the color of her eyes? What is her name? What is the name of the town?' you cannot tell me. I don't believe you are really in love with something real". Your notion of God may be vague like that, not having to do with reality. The Buddha was not against God. He was only against notions of God that are mere mental constructions that do not correspond to reality, notions that prevent us from developing ourselves and touching ultimate reality. That is why I believe it is safer to approach God through the Holy Spirit than through the door of theology. . . . Whenever we see someone who is loving, compassionate, mindful, caring, and understanding, we know that the Holy Spirit is there.

What stands out in that paragraph is the peculiarly Buddhist refusal to put much weight on *concepts*; often humorously, but always firmly, the Buddha insisted that religion is a practical business and that all concepts are more or less misleading. In setting aside the concept of "God", the Buddhist may well stay closer to the reality that the concept derives from than many of those who retain it.

Nevertheless, if we attend to Panikkar's comparison, we will reflect that the Western concept may also carry its own distinct richness and its own "take" on the truth. (In this sense, the encounter of religions is a more complex thing than the encounter between scientific theories such as steady-state and big-bang. Scientific theories can very often be set out so as to support or to contradict one another. Because of the element of translation, let alone the complexity of the concepts, this is rarely quite true of religions.)

So we might find that, although the English word "atheistic" does not really describe very accurately the Buddhist attitude to God, nevertheless something may be contained within the Christian use of the word God which the Buddhist misses, just as the swamis who welcomed Jesus Christ as the latest incarnation of Vishnu were missing something. I think that the Buddhist does miss something, and perhaps psychoanalysis can help to pinpoint it.

Pascal's "Memorial"

On Monday, 23 November 1654, shortly before midnight, Blaise Pascal, the celebrated believer that "the heart has reasons" as well as the head, had an experience that is often described as one of "revelation" or "conversion". It lasted two hours and left him filled with joy and the conviction that Jesus Christ alone was the way to God. He wrote down a "Memorial" of it on a parchment that he sewed into his clothing and that was found on his person after his death in 1662. It is not fully intelligible (Pascal, 1966, p. 309), but it begins:

> Fire
> "God of Abraham, God of Isaac, God of Jacob",
> not of the philosophers and scholars.
> Certainty, certainty, heartfelt, joy, peace.
> God of Jesus Christ.
> God of Jesus Christ.
> *My God and your God.*

What I want to draw attention to, in this profoundly moving document, are the qualifications, so to speak, that Pascal is placing upon God. He is not speaking of a God in general, nor of an intellectual construction by "philosophers" (and in this, perhaps, he agrees with the essential point in the Buddha's so-called atheism); he is speaking of the God of Abraham, and later of the God of Jesus Christ.

He is, in other words, placing himself firmly into a *tradition*, the central and powerful religious tradition that flows through Judaism and then Christianity. The God to whom he declares his allegiance is a player in particular stories and by no means a very consistent figure. Abraham related to his God in a very human way, at one point, like the travelling merchant he was, wheedling and haggling with God to bring down the number of good men required to save the wicked city of Sodom. At another point, God roundly ticks off Abraham's wife for laughing at the suggestion that she might still bear a first child at the age of 90. Later still, God makes, and then rescinds, the seemingly capricious demand that Abraham should sacrifice this much-heralded child, Isaac. The human model for this God seems to be an ultimately benign but very powerful parent who is determined not to let his son forget his dependency.

The God of Jesus Christ is a very different figure. The humour of the Abrahamic folk-tales has been replaced by much deeper moral concern; Abraham's wary distance has been replaced by a childlike acceptance, even welcoming, of dependence. Jesus addresses his God as *Abba*—"Daddy"—and he goes obediently to his terrible death "as a sheep before the shearers is dumb". Yet he can at times be impressively fierce, and some of his sayings are remarkably violent: "I bring not peace but a sword!"

The point for us here is the depth, richness, and specificity of the God that Pascal embraced. I have argued elsewhere (Black, 1993) that the contribution to religious understanding that psychoanalysis has to make lies chiefly in its notion of "internal objects", the imagined figures to which we are always unconsciously relating and which derive by a rich process of introjection and projection from our earliest experiences, even going back to the womb. Psychoanalysis speaks nowadays of "psychic reality" in order to assert that in terms of effectiveness in our lives, these figures are often every bit as powerful as those of our ordinary, external reality. It is no diminishment of religious figures such as God, Jesus, or the Buddha to say that the reality of their action for us is that of an internal rather than external object.

Gerald Edelman's (1992) account of the individual "Darwinian" development of brain structure in response to particular signals, including the responses of mother, father, siblings, and others, gives us a way to imagine *how* so-called "internal objects" become so deeply inlaid in us and why they are so stubbornly resistant to change despite all the good intentions of the conscious mind (Black, 1996).

To return to Pascal. When he embraced not simply "God" but "the God of Abraham" and of Jesus Christ, he was surrendering to an incalculably vast process. He was, above all, opening himself to an experience of love (for example, when he writes, "Joy, joy, joy, tears of joy", and later, "Let me never be cut off from him [Jesus Christ] . . . Sweet and total renunciation"). But it is love for something—an "internal object"—that is at once particular and infinite, something that takes part in specific, narratable, rememberable events and that infinitely transcends them. Perhaps, in this something, we also catch a glimpse of his lost mother who died when he was 3 years old.

In other words, the Buddha's criticism ("when I ask you, 'What is the color of her eyes?' . . . you cannot tell me") does not apply to Pascal. He had adopted a religion of incarnation, and his thinking remained as down to earth as the Buddha's. "If Cleopatra's nose had been shorter", he wrote, "the history of the world would have been different." But now he had inserted himself wholeheartedly into the story. By "believing in" these objects, he had conferred effective reality upon them (Britton, 1995). The heart had now found its reasons, and the brilliant mathematician became the brilliant religious polemicist.

This is a comparatively simple example of the transformative power of religious objects created (not from nothing), transmitted, and hugely developed within a specific tradition.

Martin Buber: God as presence

If Pascal's "Memorial", though moving, seems old-fashioned, that is because he lived before the great psychological watershed in Western history which is represented by the thought of Immanuel Kant [1724–1804]. Before Kant, it was possible for intelligent thinkers to believe that statements about the world, including religious statements, could be straightforward assertions about objective reality. Kant made the simple but revolutionary observation that the nature of experience depends also on the nature of the experiencing subject: human beings *can only* have experience if it accords with certain "categories". It must fit into the continuum of space and time, participate in the network of cause-and-effect, be of a certain intensity, and so on. At a stroke, Kant removed from us the possibility of feeling that we know reality as it is; from then on, we have known that we can only know it through the distorting filters of our subjective apparatus. (The Buddha had had the same insight 2,000 years previously; but that was still in a separate storyline.)

A direct line of descent, via Schopenhauer and Nietzsche, leads from Kant to Freud. It also leads to the religious thinker I want to speak of next, a young contemporary of Freud, also a brilliant, polyglot, Viennese Jew. He was born in 1878.

Perhaps we should start a club for those who lose their mothers at the age of 3! Martin Buber's mother abandoned her family when Martin was 3 years old. She was not heard of again for over twenty years. It turned out she had gone to Russia and remarried. Later, when Buber re-met her, he spoke of "her still astonishingly beautiful eyes" (Friedman, 1982, p. 5).

Buber rarely makes reference to Pascal. One time at which he did was when he suffered an emotional crisis at the age of 14. He found himself terrified by the infinity of the universe. He spoke of it in Pascal's great sentence, "The eternal silence of these infinite spaces makes me afraid" (Friedman, 1982, p. 27). It is tempting to link this terror at vast emptiness with the experience of loss with which both men had had to cope.

The 3-year-old Martin was taken from Vienna to live in Lemberg with his paternal grandparents. Growing up in a far more psychologically oriented world than Pascal (he was for a time a passionate Nietzschean, a lover of Goethe, and, of course, well acquainted with Freud's writings), Buber never doubted the significance of his enormous early trauma. "I have always and always looked for my mother", he wrote to his wife in his 20s (Vermes, 1988, p. 8). The philosopher who above all emphasized the importance of *presence*, of the full encounter of *ich* with *du*, *I* and the intimate *you*, the grammatical form in which a mother speaks to her child, had known almost from the outset the opposite—the terrifying, unfathomable abyss of absence.

Buber immersed himself deeply in Hasidism and Zionism, of which he was one of the early leaders. But his life's effort was above all devoted to developing his particular vision, essentially religious though not contained within any defined religion. This was of God as "presence" and of the revelatory encounter that occurs when another is experienced as You—"Thou"—rather than as he, she, or it. He writes: *"for me everything religiously actual is fundamentally a matter of the here and now, not of some historical event that is by its nature unique and incomparable"* (Horwitz, 1988, p. 113).

Immensely learned, he rejected all attempts by biology, sociology, or psychology to reduce or anatomize the absolute simplicity of the Thou-encounter. In a lecture series (out of which he subsequently wrote his masterpiece, *I and Thou*, 1970) he writes:

> The human being receives, but what he receives is not a content, but a presence, a presence as strength. [This presence includes three elements:] First, it includes the whole abundance of actual reciprocity, a state in which one is no longer cut off . . . no longer abandoned, although one cannot tell what it is to which one is linked. . . . Second, it includes—it is really the same thing, only contemplated from another angle—the confirmation of the meaning. There is undeniably a meaning, not a meaning that can be pointed out and asserted but a meaning that is thus confirmed and guaranteed to oneself, a meaning that one cannot translate. And third, this presence and this strength includes a call to the human being to put this meaning to the proof in his life through his deeds. [Horwitz, 1988, p. 115]

The language I have used in talking about Pascal, of internal objects, would have seemed to Buber to tell only one half—and the less interesting half—of the story. He knew very well that we cannot maintain our perception of the other as Thou; every Thou is fated to become once again he, she, or it (and then, at an unanticipated moment, to become Thou again), and both modes of experience are real. But it is the Thou-experience that is most precious. When I see another as Thou (or *you*, in this translation), he ceases to be *"a character to be described and experienced, a loose bundle of named idiosyncrasies. Distinct and all of a piece, he is* you *and he fills the heavens. Not as though nothing exists apart from him, but all else lives in his light"* (quoted in Vermes, 1988, p. 45). It is this sort of experience which is particularly under threat in the modern world from our scientific and utilitarian attitudes (including those that would use another for his or her own good).

The religious force of Buber's vision is very powerful. The It-world, he says (i.e. the world as understood by science including psychoanalysis, and also history, commerce, etc.), coheres in space and time. But *"The You-world does not cohere in either. It coheres in the centre in which the extended lines of relationship intersect: in the eternal You"* (Buber, 1970, p. 148). To relate to a Thou is therefore a religious experience (and I think here Buber joins hands with the Christian who says that God is love).

In a late Afterword to *I and Thou*, written at the end of his life, Buber (1970, pp. 180–181) clarified his position with regard to a personal God:

> The designation of God as a person is indispensable for all who, like myself, do not mean a principle when they say "God", although mystics like Eckhart occasionally equate "Being" with him, and who, like myself, do not mean an idea when they say "God", although philosophers like Plato could at times take him for one—all who, like myself, mean by "God" him that, whatever else he may be in addition, enters into a direct relationship to us human beings through creative, revelatory and redemptive acts, and thus makes it possible for us to enter into a direct relationship to him. This ground and meaning of our existence establishes each time a mutuality of a kind that can obtain only between persons. The concept of personhood is, of course, utterly incapable of describing the nature of God; but it is permitted and necessary to say that God is *also* a person.

In saying this, Buber retreats from his more radical earlier position, in which he once said that he believed in God when God was spoken of in the second person. But "when I speak of Him in the third person . . . my tongue cleaves to the roof of my mouth" (Horwitz, 1988, p. 153).

Religion and loss

To join a religion is to accept and to use a language that has been built up through many generations in a rich and inevitably inconsistent tradition. Religious concepts do not come naked of their histories and of their connections with the idiosyncratic individuals who have become central in the tradition—on the contrary, they have force very largely because of these specific connections. If Christianity had gone the way of Mithraism, and vanished for the past 1,700 years, it is inconceivable that the discovery today of the bare Christian gospels would lead to the founding of a major religion.

So to join a religion is also to become one of a community— some imagined group of "men of old"—who become a lively and important internal reference group. They are internalized as objects whose words and attitudes influence the believer constantly, especially at the great hinge-moments of human life: birth, marriage, the birth of children, death.

For the person who takes his faith seriously, these figures can represent a profoundly important human potential. Religious thinkers of the calibre of the Buddha, Pascal, or Buber are attempting to face the deepest reality of their human experience with absolute seriousness. They are not cutting off their emotional reactions in order to be purely "rational", nor their rational intelligence in order to dissolve in ecstasies of bliss or vehemence or loathing of self or other; they do not triumph over their sense of wonder (like the "scientistic" scientists) or over their doubt (like the fundamentalists). In their very different ways and languages, each finds, as a result of this clear-eyed, truthful search, something that energizes him and convinces him that life is worth living and that he and other people are deserving of love.

And the connection with the loss of mothers? In psychoanalytic language, we speak nowadays of the importance of the psychotic elements in the non-psychotic personality. This formula is an attempt to reach to the fact that the catastrophic un-understandable anxieties of infancy underlie and determine the psychic structure with which the child will have to deal with the passions of subsequent life, openly or defensively as the case may be. Paradoxically, it seems that in some people the necessity of coping with early loss may have creative effects. It may bring to life a need to address ultimate questions from which the less trauma-tized are more shielded. David Aberbach (1989) has demonstrated the correlation between bereavement and mystical experiences in a most impressively large number of instances.

In the past, to recognize such a correlation would have been an invitation to psychological thinkers, including some psycho-analysts, to say: "There you are! This proves that mystical experi-ence is merely a defence against mourning"; words like *denial* and *delusion* would have proliferated. We should not discount those possibilities. But it is also possible that having to cope with cata-strophic loss and aloneness compels, in some individuals, the de-velopment of resources of understanding and sensitivity which would otherwise never need to be drawn upon. Edelman's model of the formation of brain-structure, though not yet fully accepted, provides a way to imagine a very marked elasticity in human mental capacity.

The God I want

I was asked to write this essay to the title "The God I Want". Such a title might at first glance seem a trifle frivolous, an invitation to write a sort of letter to Santa Claus. But, on reflection, it is clear that the phrase contains the nub of a crucial matter.

I began this piece with the Zen aphorism: "Do not seek to imitate the men of old: seek what they sought." That is, of course, a paradox, but a wise one. It does not need a psychoanalyst to point out that seeking to imitate someone, however admirable, is likely to be a conflictual enterprise: it may facilitate identification and maturation but probably at a severe cost in guilt, resentment, and subservience. But nor can we ignore the "men of old" who, in this context, we may take to mean the people, whether in history or contemporaries, who speak to us and move us.

It is the same, really, in science or in the arts. A scientist is not just wrestling, as it were naked, with a naked problem. He is wrestling with his problem in the actual or imagined company of others (his teachers, colleagues, figures from history) and, without them, he would not even have the problem, nor the terms in which it is couched. When he writes his paper, if he is in any way serious about it and not just clocking up the score in order to be designated "research-active", he feels himself to be contributing to a tradition. The biologist is proud to stand beside Darwin, the physicist beside Einstein; or perhaps they see themselves as overthrowing these venerated figures. Similarly, any serious poet sees himself, in T. S. Eliot's phrase, as living in "the present moment of the past" (Eliot, 1953).

I said at the outset that we are now in a "new age", religiously, because the different religions now encounter one another on a footing of equality. This does not mean that they are each as good as the other, but that none has an unfair imperialistic advantage. Similarly, they now meet with science and history on the same playing-field. The tradition with which we now find ourselves in dialogue is far vaster than it was at the time of Pascal, or even Martin Buber. There is no point in our pretending to believe things that it is no longer possible for us to believe; our religion and our general world-view have to be integrated or we ourselves will be split and find ourselves speaking without firm ground under our feet.

I believe that some things—for example, a literal belief in miracles—will not survive this inevitable encounter. Such teachings must be heard symbolically or discarded. The Christian churches do themselves a disservice by their reluctance to clearly acknowledge the symbolic nature of the Christian story, including the symbolic nature of its historicity.

Some would say that the notion of God also has to be discarded for the same reason. It seems inevitably to carry, however shadowily, an image of a personal being who takes a personal interest in each one of us. In this form, it can undoubtedly foster a dangerous delusion. If God is also described as having power (even as "almighty"), it is bound to make us imagine that he will protect us. Such a God rightly attracts Freud's criticism that it springs from infantilism and the refusal to accept our own responsibility for our lives (Freud, 1927c).

However, the notion of God is not on all fours with the notion of a historical miracle such as the Virgin Birth. And we can argue that those who believe in God *are* protected in a certain way.

When Martin Buber re-met his mother, twenty years after she abandoned him at the age of 3, the word that came into his mind was *Vergegnung*, translated by his biographer Maurice Friedman, as "mis-meeting". *Vergegnung* is a neologism by Buber; however, there is also an ordinary English word that means "mis-meeting", and it is "disappointment".

One of God's functions is to provide an appointment that does not disappoint, a love, generosity, and bestowal of significance so great that beside it all our other disappointments seem minor and bearable. Those who truly believe in God are not protected from real gas-chambers, but they are somewhat protected from disappointment and bitterness and from the envy, hatred, and regret that spring from them. As it takes two to keep an appointment, this may also give an affective (and therefore effective) commitment to their principles: it is not coincidence that so many of the courageous Germans who died for resisting Hitler, including Claus von Stauffenberg, Adam von Trott, and Dietrich Bonhoeffer, were believing Christians. Finally, if they are also enabled to maintain hope, they may even cope better than the rest of us in external ("real") situations of difficulty and danger.

These strengths of the religious believer are examples of what follows from what in psychoanalytic parlance would be called the capacity to maintain a "good object", an experience of the goodness of something (most usually a person) despite its, his, or her absences and limitations. The formulation of the importance of this capacity to psychic health has been one of the crucial contributions of modern psychoanalysis. Speaking from the wider perspective of a religion, one might add: not only to the psychic health of the individual, but also to the psychic health of the society of which he is part.

Some psychoanalysts (Fromm, 1960; Symington, 1994) have suggested that psychoanalysis is really a sort of spiritual practice, because when successful it enables this capacity to maintain a good object. I think that there is a truth in this, though in my view it should not lose its primary definition as a psychotherapy. But certainly psychoanalysis can do something recognizably similar to what a traditional religion may do for someone in crisis— for example, St Ignatius after he was wounded at the siege of

Pamplona. In the prolonged process by which he transformed himself from soldier to saint, it is easy to think of Jesus Christ and the Virgin Mary, the objects of his constant adoration and remorse, as playing the role of transference figures (see Meissner, 1992). However, the great religions, including Buddhism, are unlike psychoanalysis in that they offer an account of the good object which substantiates it beyond the frail realm of contingent personal experience.

If we borrow from the Indian traditions the idea of indefinitely many levels of symbolization, then we can cope with the delusory nature of religious statements without having to discard what is true in them. "Man does not go from error to truth," said Ramakrishna, "he goes from truth to truth." The carefulness of Buber's formulation, as he speaks of his vision of God as a "person", reflects, I think, the influence of Indian thought which first entered European awareness in the century following Kant. It says: "For me, this is essential, but there are quite other ways of conceptualizing the matter which may be equally true." Panikkar, a Catholic theologian learned in the Indian traditions, with his comparison of religions to languages is making the same point.

I would add that a modern, scientific world-view need not preclude the emotions of wonder that are formative of religious feeling and vision. Science tells us that the enormous universe of which we are part has the capacity, out of barren stone and water and a handful of blue-green algae, to create, in the remarkably short time of three billion years, "the giraffe and the daffodil", Mozart and Hitler, Charlie Chaplin and the girl-next-door. No miracle story is half so wonderful as the astounding reality of this everyday world. No story of God's purposes could be more mysterious than the (probable) actuality of the "big-bang", the different generations of stars, the billions on billions of galaxies.

Thus far, perhaps, we can all go nowadays if we open ourselves to the new situation we are in and refuse the temptations of scientism or fundamentalism. In the nineteenth century, those "temptations" seemed to be the only two possibilities, and many intelligent people despaired, unable to accept the one because of its barrenness, the other because of its naivety. But the subtlety and respect of our modern thinkers, such as Buber and Panikkar, are an object lesson in holding on to the truths of experience despite the minefield of concepts, and they have shown that deep religious truth remains accessible to us without the sacrifice of our scientific world-view.

For myself, I am happiest with the language of Buddhism, which, in its simplicity and intelligence, is extraordinarily refreshing. But as Panikkar's comparison makes clear, each religion can speak of facets of the truth that others miss or under-emphasize. Christianity speaks of the preciousness of persons and personal relationships with an emotion that Buddhism cannot achieve. Judaism validates and gives shape to the world of desire as no other religion does. And, of course, each great religion now is not so much one language as a whole family of languages, some of them bearing an odd resemblance to members of quite different families (early Buddhism and Quakerism, for example).

And some religions go off the rails. We should remember the Aztecs. The Roman Catholic Church, with its disastrous imposition of celibacy on its secular clergy, has obsessed itself with sex and authority in a way that can only be called pathological.

Finally, the notion of wanting, or choice, is not irrelevant. When I spoke of von Stauffenberg and von Trott, I said: it takes two to keep an appointment. I was not referring to the actual "mis-meeting" of von Stauffenberg's attempt to assassinate Hitler, but to the humblingly courageous "meeting" that each of these men must have had with his conscience, perhaps with his God, before arriving at the decision to take such a desperate and heroic step. The question we face now, with our new religious understanding, is whether we will have a comparable capacity to choose "God", either in positive or negative form, or prefer to remain shoppers in the post-modern supermarket of abundant seductive beliefs without an ultimate coherent vision to give structure to our values. All important choice involves non-rational factors. But we need not pretend, in making this one, to be more ignorant, psychologically and in other ways, than we are.

CHAPTER TWO

In whose image?

Patrick Casement

Soul's sin is certainty, and prince's
folly is in unreflective action;
both run with pride, the decisive step,
the triumphant thought, the knowledge of discovery.

Truth then lies not in knowledge but
in doubt, wisdom in unconviction;
the strong soul is made pliable,
the weak walk forward, and are sure.

William Hillier, 1959

In writing this essay I am returning to some issues that have preoccupied me over many years. Inevitably, what I have to say will be a personal statement. I shall not be making any claim to represent the views of psychoanalysis in general or of my psychoanalytic colleagues, although I hope that some may be able to agree with what I have to say.

In a spectrum of belief, I see myself neither as a believer nor as an atheist, but as a "questioning agnostic". I arrived at this position through studying anthropology before graduating in theology. The discipline of anthropology, having opened my mind to new ways of thinking about the unknown in others, had led me to question what some might be prepared to accept on authority. In particular, I found I was no longer content with any understanding of the human condition that relied on dogma, whether that was to be found in the realm of religion or (later) in psychoanalysis. I had come to feel that everything had to be questioned, and tested against experience. (Some of what I have to say here is to be found in my chapter "Beyond Dogma", in *Further Learning from the Patient*, 1990, but here I wish to elaborate those thoughts in a slightly different direction.)

My move towards this position was expressed in one of my first publications, "A False Security?" (1964), which began with the verses I quote above. That paper was written at a time when I was undergoing what, in those days, was regarded as a "crisis of faith". I later came to realize that I had, in particular, been rebelling against the constraints of so-called certainty—towards the much greater freedom of non-certainty. (A patient once pointed out to me that, in Sanskrit, the word for "certainty" is the same as the word for "imprisonment" and the word for "non-certainty" is the same as that for "freedom". My experience amply confirms this.)

In that 1964 article I made the following statements, which pertain to the subject of this chapter:

> Few would deny that "man's heart is restless", but we must ask ourselves whether this is because he is made in the image of God, in whom some claim to have found their rest, or is it because he frets in a world that has no meaning? And is this search for meaning because there is some greater reality, which offers to satisfy it, or because life would be unbearable without some narcotic to dull the pain? [p. 29)]

and

> It may be a haven many are looking for, but they must be prepared for a precipice. For it is in our very need for a God who cares, for one who judges and redeems, and even for a heaven and a hell, that all these are suspect. So we must face the awful possibility that the God we worship may not be God at all; and even if there be a God, we may have so coloured our image of him, by our needs and desires, as to have almost

> brought him down to our own level. . . . Faith must know that
> it can never know, and must be aware of the guile of its own
> need to believe. [p. 29]

It was already dawning on me, as others (such as Feuerbach) had said before, that it is by no means certain whether we are made in the image of God, as Christians proclaim, or whether it is out of our need to believe that we may have created God in our own image. In my opinion, this dilemma cannot be resolved either by adhering to some position of religious certainty or by adopting that other kind of certainty which some atheists proclaim.

One of the responsibilities of being a psychoanalyst is to offer patients a safe and neutral space within which they can bring, and explore, whatever is their concern of the moment. And this may at times include some discussion of a patient's religious belief. More often, however, the patient is asking for help with regard to problems within themselves or in their relationships to others; and, in that request for help, they do not usually represent their religion as problematic. I therefore do not consider it compatible with my role as a psychoanalyst, as I see it, to be trying to take apart what a patient believes. Instead, I regard it as important that I can relate to each patient in terms of his or her own idiom. If that includes the patient's Catholicism, Judaism, Buddhism, or whatever, then I think it is important to learn of that, as best I can, from the patient concerned. I therefore aim to work *with* a patient's religion rather than thinking that I have any right to challenge it.

However, what I would want to question are the extremes in religion whereby a neurotic relationship to life may be mirrored in religiosity or some religious fanaticism that can become life-limiting rather than life-enhancing. But, even then, I would aim to approach the problem with respectful caution. That religious "posture" may, for instance, be the main thing that holds a person together. I would therefore want to begin the analytic task with such a patient by focusing on any day-to-day manifestations of the defensive dynamics which might also be reflected in the more extreme religious position. However, I would still not want to deprive a patient of his or her religious belief. It might happen, nevertheless, that the nature of a patient's belief matures as a result of work done in the analysis. For instance, it may become freed from the more primitive forms of religion, such as superstition, and from the various projections by which man tends to reduce his conception of God to his own image.

It is all too easy for psychoanalysts, like others, to think that they know best. It therefore disquiets me when I hear psychoanalysts being dogmatic about religious beliefs, as if these inevitably indicated some unresolved neurotic tendency in a patient which required further analytic endeavour to eliminate it. This is where I find my position as a questioning agnostic can be an advantage in my analytic practice. It helps me to preserve a neutrality with patients, whatever their religious position might be, as I do not claim to "know" either that there is a God or that there is not a God. Also, I do not think that there is one truth that is higher than all others. Rather, I have come to regard "truth", in relation to matters of the human condition, to be overdetermined—with seemingly contradictory (complementary) meanings, each having a part to play in the whole complex tapestry of life. (It has been brought to my notice that a similar idea has been asserted by Antoine de Saint Exupéry in *Wind, Sand and Stars*: "Truth is not that which can be demonstrated by an air of logic. If orange trees are hardy and rich in fruit in this bit of soil and not that, then this bit of soil is what truth is for orange trees. If a particular religion, or culture, or scale of values, if one form of activity rather than another, brings self-fulfilment to a man, releases the prince within him unknown to himself, then that scale of values, that culture, that form of activity constitutes his truth.")

It has long since struck me that people who claim to stand for "truth" frequently find themselves caught up in the primitive dynamics of splitting, denial, and projection. Whether we look at religion, politics, or psychoanalysis, we can find these dynamics operating, with schisms and sects inevitably forming as a consequence, each claiming to possess more of "the truth" than others. And it is interesting that psychoanalysts, who make a study of these primitive mechanisms of defence, can also find themselves caught up in this process. People often try to enhance their own sense of certainty as to the correctness of their own position through viewing others as being in error.

From another point of view, Isaiah Berlin, as a historian of ideas, also questions dogmatic certainty. With wry sarcasm he writes:

> Happy are those who live under a discipline which they accept without question, who freely obey the orders of leaders, spiritual or temporal, whose word is finally accepted as unbreakable law; or those who have, by their own methods, arrived at clear and unshakeable convictions about what to do and what to be that brook no possible doubt. I can only say that those who rest on such comfortable beds of dogma are victims of forms of self-induced myopia, blinkers that may make for contentment, but not for understanding of what it is to be human. [Berlin, 1991, pp. 13–14]

I wrote of this in another early publication, "The Paradox of Unity" (1963), then referring to theological schisms. But the same can apply to any belief systems, including those of psychoanalysis:

> Much of our present theological disunity may be attributable to a natural insistence upon the unity of truth. But truth, seen from the limited perspective of finite man, may not always be reducible to a single dimension. To see the wholeness of truth we may need to see the obverse side to that aspect which we can see, and contain the two aspects in paradoxical tension. [p. 8]*

And subsequently:

> In the excitement of vision, in which one sees some new aspect of truth, it is all too easy to reject the old part-truth of which this new vision is but the obverse. We tend to reject the old as totally false and acclaim the new as totally true. But truth does not lie in any single part, but in that bigger whole, which in the limitations of human perspective may only be expressible in terms of an irreconcilable paradox. [p. 8]

---

*I am not thinking here of logical truth, in which contradiction may point to some higher "synthesis" (not yet found) that could link "thesis" and "antithesis" to the point of resolving contradiction. As indicated in the quotation from Saint Exupéry, I am concerned more with personal truth that does not necessarily accede to the rules of logic.

I think that something like this happened in Freud's thinking about religion. His new understanding could be applied to so much, including the more primitive forms of religion, that it seemed to become "kosher" for psychoanalysts to regard all adherence to religious belief as neurotic. Some of it no doubt is. But I think that there is something amiss if all religious belief be regarded as suspect. And what a loss it can be if a patient's spirituality is automatically regarded as suspect by the analyst, or if a patient has to keep this away from an analysis lest it be interfered with. This is probably why so few religious people entrust themselves to psychoanalysts. And it might also be true of some analysts that they lack a proper respect for what may be the highest in mankind—a sense of spirituality—by which people can have a vision of the human condition which goes beyond the limits of an analyst's consulting-room. Psychoanalysts therefore need to be able to acknowledge that they may not have all of the answers, and that there is more to life than is contained within their particular view of it.

Being more familiar with the Christian narrative than with that of other religions, I have frequently been impressed by a resonance that is found in the human spirit with regard to what I have come to think of as the "Resurrection Principle". What I mean by this is a sequence that can be found in many areas of life whereby new life grows out of death. There are quite different ways to explain this. At an animistic level, we can see a "resurrection" sequence in the seasons of nature. Out of the dying of autumn, and the seeming lifelessness of winter, we are greeted by the new life of spring. There is no doubt that this touches something deep in the human spirit, and it is celebrated right across the spectrum of human experience: from the gardener or farmer to the poet, from painter to mystic. And of course we find it most particularly celebrated in the Christian festivals of Good Friday and Easter.

I do not know whether this Resurrection Principle is an echo of the Christian message (as some would wish to believe) or whether the Christian narrative can feel so fundamental because it parallels the triumph of new life that is found in nature, and in man's capacity to survive profound tragedy and loss. Some certainly do, eventually, rise above the collapse of all that had formerly made life meaningful. And in the course of that process there are some who feel that they find new life—deepened, even enriched, by the experience of that "death" in life. Thus, it might seem that the Resurrection Principle (as I am calling it) can be found in the consulting-room just as it may be found within a religious setting.

A further dimension to this comparison between religious and analytic experience was first drawn to my attention, many years ago, by Harry Williams (1960). He pointed out that Jesus' view of God as Father served him only up to and including his prayer in the garden of Gethsemane: "Father, if it be possible, let this cup pass from me. . . ." On the Cross, that view of God as Father was no longer adequate. What father could send his own son to be crucified? During the agony of the Cross, therefore, we hear Jesus crying "My God, my God, why hast thou forsaken me". And only later does Jesus come back to his more familiar use of "Father", in "Father, into thy hands I commend my spirit".

Once again, I do not know whether life reflects a sequence pointed to by the Christian "gospel" or whether that narrative has been so influential because others find this in their own experience too. For in the analyst's consulting-room we find patients who go through a breakdown "en route" to a breakthrough, a view of life that has previously sustained them and their own view of themselves, having since been found to be inadequate, no longer serving that purpose. For a while, sometimes for a very long while, a patient may go through the deepest despair of having lost all that had seemed to make life worth while. Gradually, however, it may become possible to look beyond that deficient vision of life to something greater. In this sense, but in the quite secular setting of an analysis, patients may go through a similar experience to that described by Harry Williams: that of going through disillusionment towards something unforeseen, which may eventually be found beyond it. [There are echoes here of similar thoughts that have been expressed over the ages, for instance: "Who going through the vale of misery use it for a well . . . they will go from strength to strength" (Psalm 84: 6); also, "the dark night of the soul" as portrayed by St. John of the Cross. In addition, my attention has been drawn to a line somewhere in Sartre, where he says: "Life begins on the far side of despair."]

But, in an analysis, I know that I cannot point any patient to what could make life meaningful for them. If a renewed sense of "life being meaningful" is ever to be adequate to a particular patient, I believe that it has to be found *by* that patient—and sometimes it is found, most tellingly.

In one sense, I find my clinical experience here to be in contrast to what I find within the Christian Church. I have heard Christians preaching "the hope of resurrection" even in the face of unspeakable tragedy. It has often seemed to me that this results, for whoever preaches it, in creating an emotional distance from the sheer pain of what another person is going through. Whilst the message surely helps to protect the preacher, it may do little for the person for whom it is intended. But a most salutary exception to this was heard during the tragedy of Dunblane in 1996 [a teacher and sixteen very young primary school children were killed in their classroom by a gunman] when so many families were shattered by the senseless shooting of their children, while parents had been thinking that their children were safe in the care of teachers whom they trusted. It was totally appropriate that a priest said, at one of the first Church services that followed: "Let there be no explanations to-day." Then was certainly not a time for anyone to take refuge from the shocking impact of that tragedy, least of all in theories trying to explain why it happened. (Psychoanalysts try to understand the perverse drives behind such a shocking event. But the pastoral task, for those most directly affected, is of quite a different order. For the bereaved, there can be no simple relief or solution to their grief, and most certainly not through "explanations" of any kind.)

Unfortunately, that is not what is most commonly preached within the Christian Church. More frequently I have heard the promise of eternal life proclaimed, and the triumph of Easter, in the face of each and every death. Some may be comforted by this. But I recently heard a friend say how unhelpful it had been for her when the priest at her father's funeral had been preaching this Easter message, and how far removed it had been from what she was going through at the time. Where, then, does this place the preacher in relation to tragedy and trauma? As an analyst, it worries me that a preacher (or a priest) can so readily take a distance from the pain of death and loss, or of breakdown, by looking beyond it to what is thought of as some resurrection promise. But a person in breakdown, or the bereaved (for instance, the families so afflicted in Dunblane), cannot take a distance from their pain. For some it will be with them for all of their lives. And it has been said that no parent ever really recovers from the death of a child. So what happens to that continuing pain for the Christian preaching of Easter? I do not believe that it is all transformed by the promise of resurrection.

I have come to think that the reflections of Good Friday (as preached) are often followed too swiftly by the Easter message. It is almost as if Christians are invited to dwell only briefly upon the death experience of the Crucifixion, then to have their attention (almost immediately) deflected from that to the promise of Easter—or so it can seem within the sequence of Church observance.

In real life, however, the Good Friday experience (of loss, breakdown, trauma, or tragedy) is seldom, if ever, so readily resolved. And, when this is encountered in the consulting-room, a patient's "Good Friday" may go on for years. The analyst's task, in my opinion, is to see this through with the patient, however long that might take. There is then no place for denial or for quick reassurance.

It has come to my notice that, when I have been able to help patients to face their own worst experiences and to survive them therapeutically, they have sometimes told me afterwards that what had helped them most had been my willingness to be alongside them during the experience. And I know that I could not really have been "with" them in this way if I had been comforting myself with the idea that they would surely come through it, as with the notion of a light at the end of the tunnel or with some other resurrection promise. For, at the time, it feels and is endless for the patient. However much I may need to believe in the possibility of some way on being found, beyond a patient's own worst experience, I know that I have to stay in touch with what the patient is going through as it is at the time. That is central to the analytic endeavour: to be sufficiently in touch with the patient's experience without seeking refuge in premature "solution".

In Christian devotion (unlike at the time of the Crucifixion), Good Friday now leads inevitably to the Christian Easter. And

every terrible experience can be reduced, even limited in its significance, by the assurance of that Easter message. There thus
seems to be a strange contradiction. The priest, whose pastoral
task includes being there for the bereaved and for those in trouble
of whatever kind, may himself be protected by his belief in the
Resurrection. This prevents him from ever being fully alongside
those he seeks to help. He may be able to give significant counsel,
but, in the last analysis, I do wonder about the gap that remains
between the priest and the actual experience of those to whom he
seeks to administer comfort. And yet, in the Christian narrative,
we are told that the function of the Incarnation and of the Crucifixion was to bridge precisely that gap: God became man that he
might enter most fully into man's sufferings, alongside him in
death as in life.

I think that we find a similar distancing in some analyses. If
an analyst places too much emphasis upon what is said, as in the
interpretations given, then something important may be missed
there too. I do not question that much of the work of psychoanalysis is that of interpretation towards patients becoming more familiar with their unconscious minds, that they may become more
able to own what is theirs and to be less prone to such primitive
defences as those of splitting, denial, and projection. But I do not
regard the analytic work of interpretation, on its own, to be
enough when trying to help a patient to live through the consequences of trauma or a patient trying to rebuild a life after breakdown. Words alone are not always enough. I have therefore come
to think that, even though analysis has been called "the talking
cure", it is not always the analyst's interpreting that is the crux of
the process. Often, what seems to be most significant to a patient
is the experience of being consistently cared for by someone who
makes it their business to get to know them as deeply as may
be—someone who is also prepared to be battered by the impact
of the patient's distress and despair whilst surviving this "without collapse or retaliation" (Winnicott, 1971b, p. 91). Something
important, and healing, can be found in the experience of the analytic relationship itself—*between the lines* of what is actually said
by the analyst—as well as in the words.

What helps to sustain me when working with a patient going
through a breakdown, or with someone who is trying to come to

terms with the experience of trauma, is the repeated discovery that some patients do eventually come through this in a way that turns out to be creative, leading even to new life and a new vision that may lie beyond anything I could have set out to convey to them. But I know that I cannot point a patient to that possible outcome, nor can I be certain if any particular patient will ever come to it. I have no guarantee, so I give none. I can, of course, call upon analytic understanding, some sense of the past that a patient may be re-experiencing in the present or some other understanding of what is happening, to help orientate me during the analytic journey. Sometimes that understanding may also help to re-orientate a patient, but there always remains a gulf between any understanding that I may *think* that I have and the patient's own experience. (I do not believe that anyone can ever entirely bridge this gap between themselves and another.) But a patient may be able to use something from what I have said, or something from my presence with them, out of which they can begin to find a bridge towards beginning to feel not so alone with what they are going through.

However, in my opinion, there is something about the analytic process that goes beyond the skill of the analyst. I do not think that it is an adequate explanation of what can happen in an analysis to imagine that it is simply a result of the work of the analyst, bringing to consciousness the troublesome aspects of the patient's unconscious mind. For if it were that alone then it would be as if the analyst were claiming to be the instrument of cure, the author of a patient's recovery. There are some parallels here to the work of a surgeon. He does not cure the patient. He may cut out what threatens a patient's life, and he carefully sews up his patient after surgery to ensure an optimum state for recovery. But the healing process lies within the patient. The analyst similarly aims to bring to consciousness what is threatening a patient's peace of mind, for patients to become able to apply conscious thought to those processes that had previously been disturbing them— beyond their ken. But a patient's recovery is never within the analyst's "gift".

I think that there are also parallels between what happens in an analysis and the relationship that evolves between a mother and her baby. When all goes well, a baby's growing security is not merely a result of the mother's skill as mother: it is not solely her achievement. There is a process that occurs between a mother and her baby whereby the baby may find what is needed. But this is not only because the mother provides it. It is through the mother developing a sensitivity to her baby's communications that she becomes able to recognize what is needed and when. Only then can her provision become meaningful. That good experience, therefore, grows out of the baby discovering that communication is meaningful and that there is someone "there" who can respond meaningfully to it. But when a mother cannot read her baby's communications, or when a baby feels that it is in a world without meaningful response, the relationship will become increasingly problematic until help from elsewhere becomes available or until the mother becomes better attuned to her baby. For good or for ill, each enhances the contribution of the other. There is a process between them that involves them both. The point I am trying to make here is that the outcome of a mother's attention to her baby, or of an analyst's attention to a patient, is not solely the achievement of the mother or of the analyst. It is a product of the two people interacting. But the mystery of it, in my opinion, may lie beyond each of them. We cannot be sure that we know what it is, in either setting, that contributes most to growth or to recovery.

Some people are particularly struck by the power of the analytic process that can develop between a patient and the analyst, and the sense of unconscious wisdom that can sometimes seem to inform this. It appears to "guide" the two people engaged in that process along a journey that could not have been devised by either the analyst or the patient alone. With hindsight, it can look as if it "had" to be that way. For instance, Winnicott pointed out the process by which the analyst finds himself subtly drawn into failing his patient in ways that uncannily re-enact a significant "environmental failure" in a patient's life. As a result, the patient often brings into his or her relationship to the analyst those feelings that belonged specifically to early trauma, with a fresh opportunity to work through that trauma within the analysis. "So in the end we succeed by failing—failing the patient's way" (Winnicott, 1965, p. 258). How does this come about? I do not know the answer, but I can understand why there are those who might be tempted to see the hand of some other force at work in this; that recovery from trauma can come about through ways that seem so contrary to common sense, and which the analyst could never anticipate or plan. (A very clear example of what I am saying here can be found in the description of my work with a patient who, in her first year of life, had nearly died of burns: *On Learning from the Patient*, 1985, chapter 7.)

I am clear that my clinical work is not conducted within any religious framework. The questions I started with remain. Do we find life growing out of death as a reflection of some Divine purpose, an echo of the Good Friday/Easter Day sequence? Or has the Christian narrative acquired such universal appeal because it dramatically portrays a sequence that already exists in life? For there is no doubt that we do sometimes encounter a process of recovery (from breakdown, from trauma, from loss) through which some people may even be transformed.

I still do not know whether we are made in the image of God or whether we have made God in our own image—or are these two views each a part of some greater truth? I am content to be asking these questions without needing any answer. Not having those answers enables me to listen to my patients from a position that is (I hope) free of doctrine or dogma that could intrude upon my analytic listening. With religious patients (of a Christian persuasion), I feel at ease in being familiar with their world-view without being committed to it myself. With the non-religious, or with those of a religious background other than my own, I am at ease in learning from them a world-view quite different from any that has been mine.

Nevertheless, whether in the realm of religion or in that other "religion" of psychoanalysis, I believe that we still need to watch for the ways in which we may devise dogma to suit our own personalities. In either sphere, our theory or our God should be as little made in our own image as can be. And if there be a God, then let that God be truly "other" and beyond our own creation—as only a true God will be. Only then might we be led to a vision that lies beyond our own limitations, as our creativity is also beyond our understanding.

CHAPTER THREE

An agnostic's spirituality

David H. Clark

I was reared in an agnostic home, and I trained and practised as a doctor for many years with no commitment to or involvement in religion. In my 50s, I became aware of spirituality in myself and in others, and I have been working on that for the last twenty years. I am no theologian, nor a philosopher, and I find lengthy discussions of these disciplines of little value. What I am offering is an account of some strange experiences in the latter part of the life of a working psychiatrist.

My father was a member of a family that had been Quakers for two and a half centuries. A brilliant scholar, he was attracted to medicine and, during his student years, became an agnostic. He left the Society of Friends but remained in contact with his many Quaker relatives. My mother was a South African school teacher who had rebelled against an oppressive Anglican up-bringing and was a committed atheist. I was born in 1920, their first child. They taught me how the world had developed, and they encouraged me to ignore the pious teachings sometimes offered at various schools. We moved to Scotland when I was 6, where I attended a grammar school as a day-boy. I showed a boyish interest in biology, and so it was decided I should become a doctor.

In my teens I read widely, particularly the romances of the great Scottish writers like Walter Scott and Robert Louis Stevenson. But I also read for myself about the world. In particular, I found the works of H. G. Wells excellent instruction. His *The Outline of History* (1920) provided a clear view of the way that man and society had developed, and he pointed out repeatedly how the ignorance and superstition of organized religion had led men into foolishness and destructiveness down the centuries.

I imbibed from my parents an ethic of social responsibility and professional commitment—the need to accept responsibility, to act responsibly, and to meet one's social commitments. Later, like all young medical students, I also wished to make people better and to make the world a better place.

Growing up in Edinburgh, I found Scottish Presbyterianism stuffy, oppressive, and narrow-minded and was mostly aware of it as a force that closed things down and forbade reasonable activities. I become combatively atheistical in school debating societies. When the Oxford Movement (Moral Re-Armament) swept through our school, I resolutely refused to have anything to do with their weekend sharing parties at which potential members were received with great friendliness and then enticed to attend meetings where people would "share" their various sins and failings.

My father retained close contact with his family, and, over the years, I came to know them well. Every Christmas we went to my grandfather's house in Street, Somerset, beside the family shoe factory. There was a great gathering, nearly all Quakers, and I became accustomed to attending Friends' Meeting. It was the only form of religious service with which I felt at ease—though often, as a fidgety child, I wished the silence would come to an end!

I studied German at school and was sent to Germany during holidays to improve my grasp of the language. Whilst visiting Germany, I met a number of committed Nazis who told me with pride of their racial theories and their plans to conquer the world; this I found repugnant, and I committed myself to the anti-fascist struggle.

I started my medical studies in 1937, aged 17, and when the war broke out in 1939, I was instructed to carry on towards qualification. I qualified in 1943 and entered the army that summer, full of zeal to do my duty and to defeat fascism. I volunteered for parachuting and saw action in 1945 in Germany and later in Sumatra. I saw the concentration camps of the Germans and the internment camps of the Japanese. I was appalled at the things that men could do to one another, and I felt a need to know more about the human mind and its vagaries. As a result, I decided to study psychiatry.

I started my psychiatric work while still in the army. In 1946, I came home, married the girl who had been waiting for me, and started postgraduate study and taking exams. I worked in Edinburgh with Sir David Henderson from 1947 to 1950 and then went to the Maudsley Hospital, where I worked with Sir Aubrey Lewis. Early on in my career, I was appalled by the state of people suffering from long-term mental illness who were locked in squalid asylums, assaulted by brutal attendants, degraded, neglected, forgotten. I studied many things at Edinburgh and the Maudsley, and undertook a personal psychoanalysis. But the desire to do something for the forgotten people in the long-stay wards remained with me. In 1953, I took the post of Medical Superintendent at Fulbourn Hospital, Cambridge, and worked there for the next thirty years.

I had the good fortune to come to Fulbourn Hospital at a time when new ideas about the care of long-term patients were on the move in Britain. I also found a hospital demoralized and wishing to change. We carried out a major programme of activity, freedom, and rehabilitation and made the hospital an "open-door hospital" by 1958. We then went on to explore many forms of social therapy, and, in particular, I helped to run a number of innovative therapeutic communities. This work received considerable acclaim. I was invited to go on lecture tours to America, Japan, Peru, and other countries. I wrote two books. I also served as an officer on national bodies and chaired a government working party.

From the time I started medicine, I had little occasion to modify my agnostic viewpoint. In the army, I met many chaplains. Some were fatuous, silly people; the best of them were earnest souls who went around trying to alleviate, ineffectively, the suffering of the wounded men. They seemed peripheral and superfluous to the grim business of battle or of treating the injured who came to us. What I saw in the concentration and internment camps led me to feel that any concept of a compassionate personal "god" who looked after individuals and intervened to care for them was arrant nonsense.

During my training years, I had little to do with clergymen, except as patients. But, when I came to Cambridgeshire, I ran into the full power of the Anglican Church in its unchallenged hegemony. It was assumed that I must be a member of the Anglican Church in good standing, and I was ordered to read the lesson regularly in the hospital chapel and to swear the oath in law courts. I found myself in revolt against these assumptions and the general arrogance, as I saw it, of the Anglican clergy. I declared myself an agnostic and insisted on affirming rather than swearing in courts of law (which got me into some trouble with irritable coroners and judges). I began to be proud of my long family history of nonconformity.

When a group of university- and townspeople got together to form the Cambridge Humanists in the mid-1950s, I was delighted to join them. I took an active part in their work, meeting such distinguished and active humanists as E. M. Forster, Edmund Leach, Christopher Morris, Fred Hoyle, Marghanita Laski, and John Gilmour. They made me aware of the long and distinguished intellectual history of Rationalism in England.

At the same time, I was meeting decent people who, because of their Christian commitment, gave a great deal of service to the mentally disordered. I gradually came to see that a compassionate desire to help other people seemed to have very little to do with a person's religious or political creed. I called myself a Socialist; yet I saw many Conservatives who devoted long periods of time to helping the mentally disordered. I called myself a humanist; but could see compassionate Anglicans and Nonconformists working with us. It was my good fortune to meet, on the hospital management committee, several admirable people who confessed that they were humanists at heart: Lady Adrian, our Chairman, Alderman Mallet, a later Chairman and Alderman Jack Warren (who had come to his socialist and humanist convictions while serving in the ranks of the regular army in India)—all admirable people who endorsed my commitment to humanism.

For many years my life and work went well. My professional work prospered, my patients did well, and the hospital became famous. I published articles and books, and our three children grew into lively adults. My wife and I had many friends and acquaintances, and an active social life. I had little to do with religious activities or spiritual concerns, and occasional brushes with local church hierarchies served only to strengthen my distaste for irrational beliefs and those who held them and persecuted others in their name.

Then, some twenty years ago, in my mid-50s, I went through a period of personal crisis. My work went awry. My professional ambitions were blocked, and I had to face a restricted professional future. Our marriage broke up, and I left my wife after twenty-seven years. I began a period of life on my own—an exciting period of sexual affairs and new beginnings. I began to explore "alternative" lifestyles, to attend strange gatherings, and to read unusual books. I took up Yoga and found many of my chronic physical ailments much improved. I began to try to meditate and attended meetings and courses, especially those teaching Vipassanah [insight] meditation.

It was at this time that I had my first clearly recognized transcendent experience. It was during a Quaker meeting. In the silence, I started to meditate. At first it was much as usual. Then, suddenly, I was filled with Bliss. It was not intense, but very good, very warming. I felt exalted, filled with goodness. I thought that this must be what "being in touch with God" must feel like. It went on for some ten minutes, then someone began to talk and it slipped away.

The following spring, I went to my first ten-day Vipassanah meditation course. I had many psychological experiences there—some of them horrid, replays of recurrent nightmares and disturbing memories—but also good, blissful experiences. After that course, I meditated in many places and every now and then had bliss experiences. I recall one on the Roman Road near Cambridge. I had been walking and then stopped to rest in the sunlight. I sat in the meditation posture, looked at the ground, and saw an ant crawling up a blade of grass. Suddenly I was the ant and the blade of grass and the wind blowing across the fields. I was filled with a glorious feeling of openness, expansion, bliss, and delight.

After each of these experiences, I would not only feel good and happy, but also greatly strengthened. I felt that I was "on the right path", that I was following a good line, and that this might lead me to something better—something that might be called "enlightenment".

I began to wonder about these experiences, particularly the striking feeling of bliss, of "oneness" with the world, of understanding, and the aftermath of happy serenity. I read Buddhist texts and read accounts of conversion experiences and ecstatic visions. In earlier years, I had read William James's *The Varieties of Religious Experience* (1902). I began to read further. I discovered that Marghanita Laski, the agnostic, had written a book, *Ecstasy: A Study of Some Secular and Religious Experiences* (1961), in which she gathered accounts of mystical experiences from many sources. I discovered Richard Jeffries's *The Story of My Heart* (1883), the nineteenth-century account of bliss experiences by an agnostic Englishman. I also came across Sir Alistair Hardy's studies summarized in *The Spiritual Nature of Man* (1979) and later works from his Religious Experience Research Centre such as *Seeing the Invisible* by Maxwell and Tschedin (1990). All these accounts convinced me that the experiences I had been having were similar to those that had happened to people of many religions (and no religion) for as long as men had made records. I realized that this was a wonderful, powerful, deeply-moving experience for which many holy men had yearned through the ages, and which the Buddhists in particular sought with diligence. It happened to people of all faiths and none, and it was not proof of the existence of any of their various gods, although many of them had felt that it was. Among professional psychologists, only Abraham Maslow (1970) seemed to have recognized what he called "peak experiences": the description matched what had happened to me.

I realized that I had had "peak experiences" before in my life. Quite often, when resting during walks, on high hills overlooking fine views, I had had periods of uplift. I remembered very clearly one such moment on a Lakeland hill, on a bleak January day in

1943, when I was suddenly filled with the wonder of the world. But I had attached little importance to these moments at the time.

I realized that some people had come to Bliss unexpectedly, without preparation. But many had been holy men who had undergone years of training, of study, of deprivation (food, sex, sleep, etc.), and even of self-mortification. All had stressed the joy, the bliss, that filled them. Many had seen, or heard, the deity in whom they believed—Christ, the Virgin Mary, Allah, Jehovah, Isis. All had emerged from the experience confirmed in their belief. They now knew that they were on the right path: their God had spoken to them and told them that they were right. Many were thus strengthened in their faith and enabled to go forward into suffering and even martyrdom. All religions had had people who proclaimed such experiences—mystics. Often they were a great nuisance to the established church because they were liable to announce that their personal revelation had shown the church to be in error. The Catholics had to burn quite a few ecstatics and, in more modern times, excommunicate them. The Muslims had to execute a number of Sufis, whilst the Puritans in England and America persecuted and even executed early Quakers.

I welcomed these experiences and sought to reproduce them. I soon found that, though I could easily attain a meditative state, Bliss was far less easily reproduced. Sometimes it came, most often it did not. I came to know what factors made it more possible and what worked against it. But it was still rare, and the more delightful when it came.

I had my first "out-of-body" experience when I was taking part in a group meditation. We were sitting in the gathering darkness of a winter afternoon. My meditation was progressing, my body was still, my breathing settled, my mind almost empty, when, quite suddenly, I felt myself moving from my body up through the room, through the ceiling, up into the air above the quadrangle. I looked down and saw my body sitting; I looked around and scanned Cambridge from the air. It was pleasant, interesting, intriguing but not particularly delightful and certainly not blissful.

I have repeated this "levitation" many times since. One of the clearest occasions was a winter's evening in Suffolk in 1980. I had been trimming a hedge and had made a fire of the cuttings. As the fire burned down to a mass of embers and darkness fell, I settled down and started to meditate. I took off and soared into the darkening sky. I scanned Suffolk and saw the sea (some fifteen miles away) and the layout of southern East Anglia. I floated for a long time, then came down reluctantly to my chilling body beside the dying fire.

I began to explore meditation further and attended other Vipassanah courses. Then, at a conference, I met John Crook—ethologist, psychologist, and Buddhist teacher—who ran five-day "Western Zen" retreats. I found these most valuable and attended several. John Crook based these on the teaching of Charles Berner who had developed the "Enlightenment Intensive" form of five-day retreat, free of religious content, designed to help people have "direct experiences" (Crook, 1990). I also attended several "Enlightenment Intensive" courses run by Jake Chapman (1988).

On one occasion, a "Western Zen" retreat of John Crook's, I experienced "Kensho"—the sudden dramatic illumination experience described in Zen writings. The first day of the retreat had been hard—the discomfort of sleeping in a tent, of rising at 6.00 a.m., of running up the hill, of pain in my legs, etc., etc. My Question (or Koan) was "What is gratitude?" The second and third days went fairly well. I took part in all the activities. My body settled down, my mind cleared, my meditation went well. "Clear mind" (empty of thinking) came quite often (and went quite quickly). I worked hard on my Question and made some discoveries about gratitude. I became aware that I felt "fortunate": fortunate in my life. I felt gratitude: but to whom? God? Christ? Allah? As I reflected on all those to whom I had been told I *should* be grateful, especially in Sunday School lessons, I got quite angry. On the fourth day, I had a review interview with John.

Immediately after this review interview, it was a work period. I found a member cleaning the Hall (Zendo) alone, and I offered to help. She asked me to shake out the mats. I took them into the courtyard and started. They were dirty and gave off lots of dust which went up my nose and into my mouth. The weather was grey but dry, and a breeze blew up in the courtyard. Suddenly I became aware! I felt myself dissolving away. I became the wind, the wind became me. I and the wind and the air and the world were all one—a great One, full of light. I knew that this was "en-lightenment". I knew that this was Kensho. It was not as full of bliss as some of my experiences, nor so full of knowledge, but it was very full of certainty and enlightenment. I saw, I knew. I had All Knowledge and All Understanding. I realized that the Question did not matter any more; it had been answered. It was over and done with.

I stood and delighted in this glory for a time. I dropped the mat and stood with open hands, full of light and delight. I felt that it would be good to stand there forever. Then the bliss began to slip, to fade. I heard the chatter of other people working in the courtyard. I felt I had better come to myself. I picked up another mat and went on with the shaking, reflecting on my amazing good fortune.

This was how I had my classic *Kensho* experience—in the courtyard of a wet and dirty Welsh farm. It had been just as in all the Japanese Zen stories: the sudden enlightenment descending in the midst of mundane work. I had never thought that it would happen to me, especially since most of my previous bliss experiences happened in special places and in special circumstances. It was amazing that it was so like what others had described.

Did this spiritual journey affect my practice of psychiatry? This is difficult to assess. I think that there was probably little difference in how I practised psychiatry but that there may have been a marked difference in how I worked with other people, both my colleagues and patients. This limited effect may be due to the fact that my spiritual journey overlapped with only the last ten years of my years of practice of psychiatry. I began to explore spirituality in my late 50s: I retired at the age of 63. Furthermore, my psychiatric work was circumscribed in those last ten years.

I had previously, for many years, seen people in psycho-therapy and often discussed their religious position. I had taken the traditional, non-judgemental, uncommitted medical position and had tried to be tolerant of all beliefs, however bizarre or re-pugnant. For the final ten years of my professional life—the early years of my spiritual growth and development—I was concerned only with a rehabilitation programme for the long-term mentally disordered, where most of my work was with nurses, social workers, and occupational therapists.

There is, however, evidence that my colleagues found me different in these later years. They told me that I was less tense, more tolerant, and pleasanter to work with than I had been. They found me more reasonable and more willing to listen to others. We had, by this time, at Fulbourn quite a few people working in the hospital who were openly engaged in spiritual journeys. A Buddhist lama was exercising his compassion as a nursing assistant on one of our long-stay wards, an Indian registrar was teaching meditation, and quite a few nurses had attended Vipassanah courses. There was a congenial atmosphere to which I responded. I cannot, however, discern any marked change in my professional practice during this time.

So what have all these explorations and experiences given me? What have I learned? How do I now regard my earlier agnostic, materialist position?

I have come to accept that there is a spiritual dimension to man's life, thinking, and feeling—that the triad of body, mind, and spirit forever interacting make the complete person. I have also come to realize that my previous "scientific", "materialistic" view was inadequate to explain how I felt and thought about myself, or to formulate adequately how men and their societies behaved. Although organized religion may be as savage, destructive, and superstitious as Wells had said, it nevertheless has its roots in a yearning that has been present in many people in all ages. The experience of the spiritual dimension of life—particularly that of mystical, ecstatic experiences in wise and influential men—has been the starting point of most of the great spiritual teachings and the major faiths.

I know that the search for enlightenment, the journey towards self-actualization, has become a major part of my life—and one of the most rewarding. Over twenty years I have sought constantly for opportunities to explore this further by reading books and attending lectures but, most importantly, by seeking occasions, teachers, and opportunities to meditate and to pursue my own path with diligence. I have found others walking a similar path—some Christians (Catholics, Anglicans, Quakers) but particularly amongst Buddhists of various sects. This is a lifelong quest which probably has no end and from which I am very easily diverted by the business of everyday life and, in recent years, by major physical illness.

Although I have moved away from simplistic materialism and acknowledged the spiritual in myself and in others, this has not changed my basic agnostic, humanist position. The very fact that these mystical states happen in all religions means to me that this is a basic human phenomenon that many people can experience—though, of course, they may deny it or ignore it, as I did in earlier years. However, the feeling of certainty that comes with spirituality may be a trap, because it makes people convinced of the truth of whatever religious myths are already in their minds. Yet nothing that I have seen or experienced has convinced me of the existence of any personal deity interfering in our lives, laying down moral laws, or instructing us in details of behaviour.

Since retirement, I have pursued my spiritual path with vigour, though physical illness in the last five years has limited more recent exploration. As my 70s pass and contemporaries die, I reflect more on my own death which cannot be far distant. In thinking of this, I find Buddhist teachings, with their emphasis on impermanence, illuminating and valuable.

Where am I now, at 77? My former simplistic materialism is not enough. Instead I acknowledge spirituality in myself and I recognize it in others, particularly in their accounts of their own religious experiences. I value greatly my "peak experiences". I feel that they have illuminated my life and deepened my understanding. I hope to progress further in my Spiritual Path. But I do not draw conclusions from these experiences of mine. I do not feel that they prove the existence of God, Allah, Jehovah, or any other supernatural entity; nor do they justify any of the practices enjoined by the believers in those entities. The experiences are for me simply an enriching mystery, a pointer to further personal growth.

CHAPTER FOUR

A good-enough God?
Some psychology–theology
crossing places

Murray Cox

The twin acknowledgement of this exploration is to both the psychological world, with its proper interest in the Mental State, and the theological world, with its emphasis on Word and Sacrament. It is my contention that each is in a vacuum without the other. They can best be brought together under the rubric of The Sacra-mental State. *Poiesis* is the third foot of the tripod which holds the other two steady, but it is not the concern of this essay until the final section.

Throughout the ensuing discussion it needs to be remembered that the language of therapy is only fully meaningful and relevant in a *therapeutic setting*. In the same way, the language of worship and the liturgy is only fully meaningful and relevant in a *doxological setting*. This calls for reciprocal respect and thoughtful observation from both sides.

Antiphon [a short piece that introduces and enforces what follows]

To open one publication by quotation from another might seem to be the refuge of the creatively destitute. But it is also a way of quickly establishing a frame of reference and bypassing explanation.

> Towards the end of a therapeutic group in Advent, with its wide ranging reflections upon the word becoming flesh and words spoken by "the voices", one patient turned to me and said:
> "It'll soon be Christmas in Broadmoor."
> "Just in Broadmoor?"
> "Yes . . . Bethlehem is *still* a place . . . isn't it?"
> The concreteness of precise location, "Bethlehem is still a place", can be seen as a "disturbed" patient's way of cutting through layers of irrelevant philosophical abstraction, which distracted her attention from the one fact of which she needed to be certain. She knew that Broadmoor was still a place. That Bethlehem was also still a geographical location was what mattered. Historically and theologically, the first Christmas was indeed remarkably localized. [Cox & Theilgaard, 1987, p. 247]

These events really happened—an admission to Broadmoor and a birth in Bethlehem—"and they gather round them all the inscrutable mystery of life and death and time" (Humphreys, 1968, p. 269).

The *skandalon* of the particular always causes a collision that can never be avoided in any discussion involving Christian theology in general and Christology in particular. But the most fascinating "necessary collision" is between the *psychoanalytic developmental line* (A. Freud, 1966, p. 62) and the *theological redemptive line* (Cullmann, 1951, p. 107). We all progress or regress along the former depending upon the resilience of our inner objects and the force of external challenges. Our redemptive accessibility is likewise dependent upon inner and outer constraints. An absorbing question is the degree of inherent adaptability at that inevitable point of intersection when and where the developmental and the redemptive lines meet. They also stand vicariously for the *Weltanschauung* of psychoanalytic psychology and theology, respectively. In the words of Robert Graves (1961):

> *That startle with their shining*
> *Such common stories as they stray into.*

Startling shinings

I suggest that this is a two-way process, and that the startling shining that may imply illumination and insight is no respecter of person, psychological "school" (developmental line) or religious tradition (redemptive line). *"We're here for you"* was said by one patient to another in a Broadmoor group. Without doubt this was a "startling shining" which had strayed, unbidden, into the group. It carried infinitely more therapeutic weight than anything said by a professionally trained, formally designated, "therapist".

There are complex conscious and unconscious processes unleashed in the development and resolution of psychotherapeutic transference phenomena. How much more daunting are the existential obligations called into activity by that other pervasive transference re-enactment evident in theories of the atonement. Guilt and internalized grace can yield to subsequent startling shinings. An individual may well find it hard to say whether a religious experience or a psychotherapeutic shining, after prolonged and unimaginable darkness, is the more startling. An understanding of their integration is perhaps the most startling thing of all.

Preamble

The fundamental problem is to know when a mutually acceptable area of common ground, on which psychodynamic psychology and theology can comfortably stand, has been established. The possibility of appearing patronizing, by "explaining" the self-evident, is as great as that of assuming familiarity with an unknown landscape.

Our understanding of human nature would be immeasurably impoverished were Freud, "and all his works", suddenly to vanish from the face of the earth. Psychoanalytic psychology has much to say on the importance of holding and being held, initially by a mother and subsequently by those other holdings that afford safe emotional anchorage. This means that it can also explore the sequelae of a break in the containing or a breakdown in the holding capacity of the mother, a therapist, an institution or that of a wider cosmos still. Furthermore, psychoanalytic theory can help us to understand the religious colouring of much psychopathology and the distorted psychological contours of much religious pathology, as well as every kind of sexual–religious perversion.

The very title of this chapter exemplifies the discriminating power of *allusion*. To the initiated, it invokes Winnicott. To others, it does not. Missed allusion is one of the inherent poverties that characterize much psychology/theology debate. By definition, we recognize allusions that are "apparent". But we do not know how many we miss. Clinicians fail their patients when failing to ask themselves what they might be missing, what "else" they might be seeing. Psychology and theology may equally fail each other— and, in so doing, themselves—by failing to answer the invitingly reciprocal question: *"What seest thou else, In the dark backward and abysm of time?"* (*The Tempest*, I.2.49, emphasis added).

It is often claimed that the quality of our parenting—our mothering and our fathering—more particularly, whether it is "good enough" or not—determines through projective magnification whether or not God (should he exist) could be good enough. Psychobiography may help us to understand why God is sometimes perceived as a fierce implacable tyrant and sometimes as an over-indulgent nurse. The reductive core at the heart of the analytic process can certainly give a running commentary on the kind of God that a man might long for at different stages in his journey along the developmental line. But it has no relevant authority to give it any kind of ontological grip on whether, or not, "heaven cannot hold, nor earth sustain" the God about whom many sing in the bleak mid-winters of human experience, when loss, abandonment or frozen introjects prevail. What psychoanalysis cannot do is to add a cubit to the stature of the ontological validity of religious phenomena *per se*. It is not equipped to speak for or against the autonomous ultimacy inherent in the experience of man's encounter with the God of Abraham, Isaac and Jacob.

During the last thirty years I have had the privilege of being gradually allowed into the inner world of many people. Here theology and psychology are at one facing the *mysterium tremendum et fascinans* and its concrete specificity. *The intersection of the developmental line and the redemptive line has already been mentioned. It is one of the most challenging conceptual concerns this essay can present.* Prolonged supervision in each discipline only serves to highlight this creative tension. We shall also be exploring many of the parallel patterns and confluent concerns that both therapeutic and religious experience carry.

Amble [to proceed at a leisurely pace]

Apart from the certainty that I could never do justice to such important cross-currents of thought, experience and behaviour, I felt that the best way of attempting this seemed to be that of describing three recent incidents, which were thrown into focus by the editor's invitation to contribute to this volume. That things poetic, clinical, and theological seem to be inextricably interwoven is something that I have knowingly sensed, as certainly as I know anything at all.

1.   During a performance in The Other Place [The Royal Shakespeare Company's small experimental theatre at Stratford] of the medieval morality play *Everyman*, a female actor in a diaphanous black dress entered and gyrated seductively before Everyman, who was played by a solitary male actor. His evident excitement grew, and she became increasingly irresistible. She then announced that she was Death and kissed him passionately. Shortly after this, another figure—also in black clothing—entered and made the following announcement:

     "Ladies and gentlemen, I regret to have to inform you that one of the actors has had an accident and we are unable to continue with the performance. In The Other Place we do not have understudies."

This message is clearly of vast existential significance. In encounter with death, there never can be an understudy.

2. Many of the patients in secure psychiatric facilities are those whose index offence is arson. It is an exceedingly dangerous initiative to "light just a small fire", which so often becomes out of control. The ferocity and fascination of fire, its power to warm and to destroy, is of relevance to all—psychoanalysts, poets, fire-fighters, forensic clinicians and lawyers. On 10 January 1997, I had set aside an afternoon to explore the power of the poet's incandescent image, to move through the concrete forensic relevance of fire to the dynamic implications of its religious significance. The time frame within a course at Stratford had been jealously preserved, as had the secure privacy and quiet of a hotel room. I was literally just applying pen to paper to write on the efficiency of fire as a religious metaphor, when my quiet solitude was shattered by a deafening and exceedingly effective fire-alarm bell just above my head!
    "This is not a test. We have to evacuate the building immediately."

3. In The Other Place, I was present at a newly created version of the Medieval Mysteries. It was the day after the opening night of *The Creation*. An entirely naked Adam and an entirely naked Eve, unembarrassed and relaxed, ambled across the small dramatic space, listening to God, who told them of the tree of the knowledge of good and evil. But when God left them on their own and they had eaten of the forbidden fruit, they covered their genitalia with leaves, looking as uncomfortable as any of us might, being naked at the focal point of 170 pairs of eyes and illuminated by spotlights. Their ambling ceased abruptly and they ran out. Shortly after this Cain killed Abel.

These episodes in turn bring us face to face with the fact that we have no understudy who can face death for us, that great is the confusion if there is failure to distinguish between metaphorical and concrete statements and, finally, that from mythical, primordial origins there can spring "the first founding murder and the first biblical account to raise a corner of the curtain that always covers the frightful role played by homicide in the foundation of human communities" (Girard, 1987, p. 161).

The clock-face

In order that clarity of presentation prevails, I have adopted the verbal logo of a clock-face. This symbol, reminding us of the important march of time, which is both linear and circular, demarcates twelve sections, each dealing with a crucial theme. Perhaps another reason for using the circular clock-face idiom is to emphasize that all points on the circumference of a circle are equidistant from the centre, just as all points in time are equidistant from eternity. The figures on the clock-face have also given me freedom from having to rank my chosen themes in order of relevance. All are necessary. However, an enterprise of this nature is inevitably a condensed amalgam. Many key theological concepts—such as *aporia (a perplexing difficulty), eschatology (study of the four last things), chronos* and *kairos*—which have such a direct bearing, particularly on forensic psychology, have had to be ignored. A more comprehensive consideration entitled *In All These Things* is to be published elsewhere, together with a supportive bibliography.

I. Beginnings and endings

For three reasons, 1967 seems to be a good year from which to start. First, in that year, I read a newly published book, *The God I Want* (Mitchell, 1967). Curiously enough, I recently came across it and was thinking how much I would enjoy the challenge of trying to formulate such a personal *credo*, when the editor asked if I would like to do this very thing!

Second, after ten years as a general practitioner in North London, drenchingly psychologically baptized with all the psychodynamic ramifications with which individual, familial and societal life teems—and equipped with the Diploma in Psychological Medicine—in 1967 I started full-time psychiatric work. This was soon to include sessions as a visiting psychotherapist to H.M. Prison Pentonville and as Lecturer in Forensic Psychiatry at the London Hospital Medical College, a post linking the Departments of Forensic Medicine and Psychiatry. I was astonished to hear Professor Desmond Pond, an acknowledged authority on brain damage, refer to an adolescent patient who "seemed to be suffering from ontological insecurity and existential anxiety", thus introducing me to Tillich's (1951) terminology.

Third, there is something about the unfolding personal journey along a professional developmental line which not only makes its mark, but also exerts some inner pressure that says "set this down". The ageing process—which at least in part of its journey is also a maturing process—makes its mark.

II. The vital balance

It is not easy to judge the best balance between the opposing excesses of too much or too little autobiography in a work of this kind. That I am writing as a psychotherapist and a psychiatrist, 65 years old, is a significant fragment. At various points in my life when I was, for a while, "running alone", I subsequently found myself running alongside those deeply immersed in the related disciplines of literature, language and theology. When I use the word theology and refer to my personal involvement with it, I am inevitably referring to Christian theology, Christianity being the only religion I know from the inside, although it is of course richly embedded in the whole Judaeo–Christian tradition. Such Christian theology, in rudimentary form, was there for me in phase-specific form from the cradle onwards. My father was a Methodist minister who loved language and was at one time a university teacher in Hebrew. My mother was a good-enough mother. I have no doubt that her safe holding and "watching each phase unfold as it came", and my father's more distant questioning, have had much to do with a sense of feeling "safe when all safety's lost".

At Cambridge I was officially reading Medicine, but most of my friends were reading English, so that the poetry of Housman and Yeats was as familiar to me as was my knowledge of the various foramina in the base of the skull. At my recent 65th birthday celebrations, a contemporary (with justified poetic licence) said: "When Murray was handed a skull during the final anatomy viva and asked to comment on it, he replied: 'Alas poor Yorick! I knew him Horatio'" (Hamlet, V.i.203).

For me, even as an amateur, theology was and has remained the most exciting and tantalizing of all disciplines. Maybe its inherent quality is that of disturbing hitherto established balances. "Theology's business has always been the transgression of boundaries. It is a discourse which requires other discourses for its very possibility" (Ward, 1996, p. 1). The conceptual sparking gap between Transcendence and Immanence is one that can never be dismissed as it impinges upon every human encounter. Thus, by definition, its energizing and evocative affinities permeate each individual and group therapeutic session, just as much as any formal religious gathering.

The efficacy of this essay in linking the worlds with which it grapples, and even their interpenetration, depends upon attaining an optimal point of balance.

III. The language of authenticity

At one stage I was supervised in theology by John Austin Baker, subsequently Bishop of Salisbury, who wrote "When God enters our space and time, a man is what he becomes". He was constantly stressing that we should think about "How in the context of God and of the nature of Man, as God has created him, we should take charge of our own becoming, to decide where we really want to go" (Baker, 1970, p. 358).

In 1976, I showed him a series of 280 disclosures that I felt had the quality of a nuclear disclosure, which is to say that each had somehow captured the essential existential predicament of the patient at the moment of utterance. John said that he found them "absorbingly interesting", and it seemed ages while he re-packed and lit his pipe before he said *why* they were so interesting, Then followed a sentence that is etched in my memory (Cox, 1978, p. 221):

> *Never engaging with the present moment is a recurrent theme* ...
> for the authentic person conditions never have to be right.

Authenticity may be setting-specific, within *a therapeutic setting* or in a *doxological setting*. Either way, I have always taken seriously what people say, and I always will. In 1982, I published "I Took a Life because I Needed One". There is a curious perversion at work when taking the words of a patient seriously (particularly if they have the qualities of a nuclear disclosure) is described as being "brilliant"—especially when it is simply saying exactly what the patient said! Whilst the statement has implications about the dynamics of a psychotic assailant, it also carries theological implications about the human predicament. This is the *aesthetic imperative* (Cox & Theilgaard, 1987, p. 21) in action, and it exemplifies the way in which things clinical and things theological can throw light upon each other.

IV. The salient search

My salient search was for a setting and arena where the patient's experience, and the language he used to describe it, were taken with the utmost seriousness. There was no doubt that hearing and receiving the patient's chosen language of disclosure in the major experiences of birth and death are part of the daily life of a general practitioner. However, I wondered whether academic psychiatry was the setting I was really looking for. It was, therefore, somewhat disappointing to discover that although phenomenology was regarded as important, technical terms *about* what the patient had said seemed to carry more weight than the "things themselves".

I therefore decided that depth psychology, which to me, then, meant primarily Freud and Jung, must be the arena that dealt most explicitly with the patient's language. But here, again, there was only a partial answer. To my young trainee ears, there seemed to be some imbalance between the profusion of technical terms, which any new discipline quite justifiably demands, and their failure to facilitate closer engagement with what the patient was saying! Indeed, there were many parallels not only between the specialized vocabulary, but also the diary-filling series of evening meetings, seminars, planning groups and the like that, to me, were so similar to the denomination-ridden lifestyle in which I had grown up. It was just that terms such as Baptist, Methodist, or Anglican were replaced by Freudian, Kleinian or Jungian.

I eventually came to realize that the universal language of the poet, which could be interpreted by Baptists, Methodists, Anglicans, Freudians, Kleinians and Jungians alike, was what I had been seeking. It was the latent "poetic" *in each patient* that proved to be decisive, because *timbre*, rhythm and cadence augment *attunement* to cognitive–affective disclosure. And, paradoxically, to silence too.

V. Limit situations

The fact that both theology and forensic psychology impinge upon the relevance of appropriate action in the extremity of limit situations (Tracy, 1981, p. 4) is one reason why they have so much to give each other. Perusal of my published work in forensic psychotherapy will confront the reader with many limit situations where love, hate, life, death are of the essence (see also "The Nearness of the Offence", Cox & Grounds, 1991). Furthermore, such a situation is not merely a reactivation of a primal scene or an assaultative constellation. It can arise in the therapy session *de novo*.

The search for authority is often called into question in critical, existential limit situations. Theology and psychology exhibit interesting correlations here. "The Bible Says" or "Mother Church Teaches" are the Protestant and Catholic authorities, respectively. In psychodynamic clinical work, "where '*is*' this in Freud, Klein, Winnicott etc.?" is often asked—"How do you *know*?" And the answer that a patient is being taken at his word seems to carry less credence than an identical quotation from a publication by a recognized "authority" on what one of *his* patients once said! Less credence perhaps, but surprise nevertheless that "I took a life because I needed one" should be uttered in therapeutic space. Limit situations are re-enacted there, and the authoritative stamp of lived experience is evident. Many are the reasons why so little has reached "the literature".

VI. Deictic stress

Deictic stress is the term used to describe enunciatory emphasis—a statement can "say" several different things depending upon inflection and weight. It is something that tips the balance of meaning in virtually every social encounter, from the trivial domestic exchange to the most profound stammering diction by a deathbed. For example, in Ibsen's *John Gabriel Borkman*, both women involved with Borkman use words with such differing deictic stress. One says "He was a *great* man", to which the other replies "He *was* a great man".

It is with actors in rehearsal that I have been most aware of the importance of the issues involved, and a sense of time well spent when endeavouring to ascertain just what it was that was being said, when the text came alive in the spoken word. I am aware that to be present during the rehearsal process is as much a point of privileged access as it is to be in a therapy session. The therapist is always in such privileged proximity to the inner world of another, who is struggling with what he cannot quite say. The theological link to deictic stress is not only the power of the spoken word; it is also the core concept and conception of words doing things. Becoming flesh.

Phatic and *Apophatic* language are linked to the establishment of attachment or its relinquishment. Both circle round the epicentres of Intimacy and Ultimacy. *Phatic* language, in which psychological *contact is more important than the content*, is vital in establishing early mother–infant bonding, whereas *Apophatic* language is often a feature of religious discourse and conveys a kind of ironic denial—a "speaking of or away from". The clinician will immediately tune in to the theme of "talking past the point". *Christianity and the ideal of detachment* is a theological pull that calls for discussion and on which Rowan Williams (1979) has written, whereas *attachment* is a current clinical centre of interest and research.

VII. The particularity of predicament: a handful of nails

In Broadmoor, it was once the annual practice to perform a pageant in the Chapel during Holy Week. Patients seriously rehearsed their roles to form the conventional cluster of people who mocked, assisted or merely watched while Christ slowly trod the steps of that unparalleled developmental line, the *Via Dolorosa*. During the year in question, the rehearsals had gone without fault. But, when it came to Good Friday, the man who played one of the junior soldiers due to assist in the crucifixion became acutely anxious, even though he knew his lines and knew exactly where to place himself during the pageant, carefully clutching a handful of nails. With a look of regret, as though something was beyond his manual and intellectual grasp, he whispered to the religious director—"These nails won't do. They are too short for the crucifixion."

There was no risk to security, such as a literal enactment. Instead it brings metaphor into the picture. It is a warning about the dangers of sudden islands of concrete thinking in a psychotic patient whose capacity to conceptualize and think metaphorically had been temporarily relinquished because of exposure-engendered anxiety. It was not that he would *really* crucify his friend who was playing Christ, but that he would let the team down. His self-esteem regulation plunged for a moment, until all those fellow travellers on the Via Dolorosa were able to reassure him that their joint undertaking would be the "success" that careful rehearsal had justified.

Psychological growth and integration cannot avoid some private journey along a way of sadness. The Dolorosa aspect and the need to tread carefully could, in my view, apply equally to the way in which the world of psychoanalytic psychology should address those for whom the Incarnation is the greatest truth they will ever know, and vice versa. This makes "inclusive" psychological statements about a Christian "position" untenable. Religious "dismissals" of psychology are equally invalid. Reciprocal ripeness is all.

VIII. Polarities

The temporal and spatial polarities of Now and Then, Here and There are universals—as are Eternity and Infinity. Psychiatric clinicians are used to debating whether or not a particular patient is suffering from a bipolar affective illness, and polarities are evident in many forms of rating scales and typologies. Likewise, it is impossible to start reading theology without coming face to face with an interlinking series of polarities such as Transcendence and Immanence, Love and Wrath, Justice and Mercy, Majesty and Meekness (Carman, 1994).

As Tillich (1951, p. 3) observed in his *Systematic Theology*, "Theology moves back and forth between two poles, the eternal truth of its foundation and the temporal situation in which the eternal truth must be received. Not many theological systems have been able to balance these two demands perfectly". Tillich believes that "Christian Theology is *the* theology in so far as it is based on the tension between the absolutely concrete and the absolutely universal". And later on he writes: "There is only *one* genuine paradox in the Christian message—the appearance of that which conquers existence under the conditions of existence. Incarnation, redemption, justification, etc., are implied in the paradoxical event. It is not a logical contradiction which makes it a paradox but the fact that it transcends all human expectations and possibilities."

Polarity is also evident in relation to Holy Ground and Sacred Places. Is a place only "Holy" because it is a "Holy Place", such as Jerusalem? Or is there another existential reading of "Holy Place", as being what it is because it is the site where deep human encounter takes place. A sacramental view of therapy, where therapeutic space itself is the kind of place where Oedipus took off his shoes, may facilitate some of the deepest intrapsychic transmutations.

Berkhof, a Dutch theologian, writes (1986):

> With Abraham begins the awareness of a break between the deity and the experiential world. Religion loses its self-evidence. God is now far away and hidden. But when he comes and helps, he is infinitely closer than any God of naturalism could be. Then he has a face, then he has an unambiguous purpose, then he is present as the great covenant partner, and it takes the most daring anthropomorphisms to describe his saving nearness. [p. 15]

The last two words resist psychoanalytic appropriation, whereas *therapeutic proximity* does not (Cox & Grounds, 1991)!

IX. Congruous polarities

In 1973, I wrote "Dynamic Psychotherapy and the Christian Response: Areas of Congruence". I recall the excitement of suddenly realizing that the two main emphases of the Gospel were remarkably congruent with two of the main psychotherapeutic emphases. The problem confronting me then was to find a suitable language that would be acceptable in each territory. I imagined asking agnostic or atheist therapists how they would classify the two main psychotherapeutic needs of the majority of the patients who had consulted them.

I suggested that the main psychotherapeutic thrust would be towards an analytic (exploratory, self-confrontational) approach on the one hand, and a supportive one on the other. The latter would be appropriate for those whose personality structure was fragmented and precarious, and whose self-esteem was minimal; their fragile defences would need buttressing and reinforcing by every kind of supportive therapeutic initiative that a therapist could appropriate. The former, however, would be those who needed the challenge and demand of augmented self-confrontation to relinquish maladaptive and primitive defensive mechanisms and integrate a richer affective life with higher levels of self-esteem regulation.

The central tenets of the Gospel, when thinking of the impact that encounter with Christ made, could also be seen in terms of both support and confrontation. Quoting from the Gospels, we could say that the two germinal dominical texts that illustrate this polarity are as follows:

"Come unto me" [Matthew 11: 28]
"Come follow me" [Mark 8: 34]

It is immediately apparent that the first is congruent with the supportive energies of psychotherapy, whereas the second is the demanding, self-analytic confronting of self at depth where primitive defences are restrictive and diminishing. The first embraces the nurturing, consoling, accepting, non-judgemental characteristics of love. The second indicates the capacity to respond to confrontation, challenge, and commitment—indeed, love in a different key.

The interesting philosophical, one might say psycho-energizing, dynamic behind these two congruent polarities is of course the pivotal topic. Another interesting polarity is the resonance between the capacity for *Intimacy* and that for *Ultimacy*. They are aligned with *alterity*, and the concept of the familiar stranger within oneself, and so invoke Buber and encounter with Levinas.

X. Incongruous polarities

There are areas of experience in which I think Christian theology and practice are out of step with the reality of clinical experience, and it is retreatist to ignore them. They are in evidence again and again when human beings experience loss. I suggest that most Christian practice does not allow adequate time for the lostness of loss to register. People are numbed and disbelieving, not only in the sudden bereavement due to an unexpected road accident, but even at the long-anticipated death of someone with terminal carcinomatosis. The actual impact of the absence of the often annoyingly familiar "small change" of human encounter—a particular glance, a figure of speech—has yet to be registered: the fact that he who is dead *has* died.

The funeral ceremony itself is a psychologically valuable *rite de passage*, serving the vital function of reinforcing evidence that the person is indeed dead. What is psychologically wrong is the confusing simultaneous participation in two different time frames which is implicit in the Christian funeral service: "I am the Resurrection and the Life." It gives a sense of rushing from this life to the next, without the possibility of the slow gradually cumulative acceptance and realization that the bereaved has "crossed over". In my experience as a GP, as well as the far fewer experiences of personal family losses, I am bewildered when I hear the momentous words of the funeral service rushing me from stage to stage, long before I am psychologically ready for them. It is impossible to come to terms with psychologically, however wonderful the promised developmental counterpoint and harmonies may be. At such times, silence may be the best form of counselling. As Emily Dickinson put it in a letter: *"It was too soon for language."*

There are several other areas of psychological veracity which are at odds with much traditional Christian teaching. The psychological relief that sacramental confession offers is beyond doubt. But it is simply not true to claim that the priest who hears confession is always untouched by what he hears. Each denomination has its strength and its weakness. And those with particular affiliations will know what they are, in the same way that psychoanalysts and psychotherapists trained in different traditions/schools will know what their strengths and weaknesses tend to be.

XI. On the Shoulders of Giants (OTSOG)

Freud's status as a pioneering giant is unassailable, and Wallace (1991) gives us an excellent overview of psychoanalytic perspectives on religion. The splendid acronym "otsogian" comes from the title of Merton's 1993 book *On The Shoulders of Giants*. Merton is a sociologist to whom I have always been grateful for his typology of human interaction, which I set alongside a psychodynamic perspective when assessing an individual's mental state and his capacity for social interaction. William Graham writes of the "Otsogian" critical apparatus: "Indeed, the extensive notes are a fair indication of the gigantic and the lesser shoulders whose support afforded me vistas of territories I could never have surveyed without them." I have borrowed these words from his preface to *Beyond the Written Word* (1987, p. xii) and enjoy discussion about the impact of theological fields of study on related territories.

I find retreat from interdisciplinary dialogue utterly inimicable to the search for truth, which must be integrated and integrating if it is to mean anything at all. It was for this reason that I requested as my "one luxury" at the end of the 1990 Foulkes Lecture (Cox, 1993) that, in addition to the Bible and the collected works of Foulkes, there might be a serious debate between those representing theology and the world of psychotherapy. This sense of inner safety when asking "cross-border" questions must partly stem from good-enough introjects and partly from the theological and clinical giants on whose shoulders I first peered into the "secrets of the deep". It seemed sad that one needed to make a plea to avoid the patronizing attitude of unilateral "sniping at the enemy" which has so often taken the place of the potentially rich and diverse interdisciplinary dialogue.

A true intellectual "giant" was Charles Raven, a Cambridge Professor of Divinity. I was fortunate to be a medical student at the time when he was at the culmination of his career in Cambridge. He claimed that it was impossible to talk about theology without knowing about the evolutionary process and as much biology as a layman could imbibe. His intellectual grasp and detailed knowledge of zoology and botany was mind-blowing to me as a student. It is scarcely credible that a Professor of Divinity could, at a moment's notice, be asked to stand in for a Professor of Botany who was suddenly taken ill and to lecture—using Latin names—without notes.

What has this to do with the title of this chapter *A Good-Enough God?* Paradoxically, we seem to have gone some way to answer Tertullian's impassioned cry—"What has Athens to do with Jerusalem?—The academy with the temple?" (Whale, 1967). It is a plea for deepening exchange between psychology and theology. I remember Raven preaching in 1949:

> The rocks are full of the fossils of great creatures which had so much protective armour that they became insensitive to changes in their environment and so perished. . . . So it is possible that the same may happen to the church when it becomes insensitive to environmental changes which are necessary for its continued vitality.

Could this carry a coded message for us here and now, in terms of the disciplines under discussion?

XII. Habitable bridges: paradox and hope

Bridges are "in". On my desk at this moment are four publications about bridges. The first is a book I am looking forward to reviewing: *Bridges: Metaphor for Psychic Process*, by Rosemary Gordon. There is a "flyer" about a major international conference on the psychotherapy of schizophrenia entitled: "Building Bridges". There is also the catalogue of a current exhibition at the Royal Academy of Arts: *Living Bridges: The Inhabited Bridge.* And there is a 1995 inaugural lecture by George Rousseau on *Bridges of Light: The Domain of Literature and Medicine.*

The theme of habitable bridges—bridges in which one can live and move and in which both psychology and theology can have their being—seems to be an appropriate end to this journey round the clock-face, before we return to Beginnings and Endings. The habitable bridge across which we can travel both to Endings and Beginnings is built on the twin-pillars of Paradox and Hope. It is also a vigorous *mutative metaphor* (Cox & Theilgaard, 1987).

This is a personal view, but one that has proved reliable—especially in that acute and unavoidable confrontation with self when therapy involves both literal and metaphorical wounding, disfiguring and killing. Had this essay been written after working in forensic psychotherapy for six months, it could not carry the weight of hope or its incipient *frisson* of paradox which the extended experience for a quarter of a century can vouch for. Hope, according to Kierkegaard, is a passion for what is *possible—not* wishing for the *impossible*. It is intrinsic to a *sacramental* view of life.

Poiesis: the central axis

It may seem strange to find that the central axis upon which the hands of the clock rotate is polished and preserved by poetry. Or, more precisely, by the process of *poiesis*, which is the calling into existence of that which was not there before. The "pull of the primordial" is a recurrent theme in Cox and Theilgaard (1987, 1994). It is inherent in the power of the poetic, and it characterizes the deepest personal disclosures, which are often best facilitated within a religious or therapeutic setting. Within psychoanalytic psychotherapy it can mobilize augmented aesthetic access to the heavily defended personality. Yet, for centuries, it has been an intrinsic part of religious experience. This is a primordial encounter in which renewal of every kind is possible—including the guts and grace that enable those in therapeutic and doxological settings to endure *The Dark Interval* (Crossan, 1988).

If Hope and Paradox focused in *poiesis* are found at the turning centre of the these reflections, it has something to do with the creativity of continuous surprise whenever new categories, or wider frames of reference, present themselves as being reliable. Hope in a "hopeless" situation does just this. And one of the many centralities of the Incarnation is not that the Good-Enough God "knows" *about* the storm, but that he is *part of* the storm. This applies to both the intrapsychic storms and those in the outer world which both psychology and theology address. Murray Jackson and Paul Williams (1994) describe psychoanalytic psychotherapy with psychotic patients in *Unimaginable Storms: A Search for Meaning in Psychosis*—a title that speaks for itself. *Naming The Whirlwind* (1969) and *Reaping The Whirlwind* (1976) by Gilkey are two theological works born to form a trio with *Unimaginable Storms*.

Attempting to deal with a theme of this enormity, one is inevitably doomed to failure. When we try to bring together thought on religion and psychotherapy, we soon run out of adequate conceptual language and reach the point described by States (1978) where we approach "depth which articulation would only violate".

There is a kind of baffling certainty about the richly textured link between the centrality of the cross in Christian theology and the reliably inscrutable depth of the unconscious in psychoanalytic psychology. Maybe I have been writing of a God enough Good all the time. But, then, "Some Crossing Places" was part of the title. And should it all prove to be a *Folie à Dieu*, the title of John Austin Baker's 1970 book could not be more appropriate.

CHAPTER FIVE

Psychotherapy and religion

Patrick Gallwey

It is often maintained, usually by those who have little real understanding of the subject, that psychoanalysis is a religion. By this is meant not simply that psychoanalysis is unscientific, but that its practice relies on blind adherence to a doctrine and set of tribal rituals. Having had much religious indoctrination in my youth and later trained as a psychoanalyst, I thought it might be interesting in this contribution to reflect on how far this is true, and to what extent psychoanalysis as a body of thought and practice overlaps with religion and where it is in opposition.

Straight away one is up against the reality of such a task in so far as religion is an extremely diverse and complex set of practices and beliefs, and library shelves groan under the weight of psychoanalytic writings. I am not therefore going to attempt to define either but trust that the way I am using the terms becomes clear as we proceed. I am also going to confine my discussion to two areas: the question of good and bad behaviour, in other words morality; and the issue of life after death, which in many ways is bound up with morality since most religions promise it as a reward for good behaviour. It will always remain a puzzle as to why anything exists at all. Morality and immortality do not follow necessarily from belief in a Creator and, if anything, tend to recede as the argument from design becomes more compelling with the advance in our understanding of the origins of the universe. (This issue is discussed very fully in Davies, 1992.) Any creator emerging from the ability of the human mind to construct a mathematical model of the origins of the universe would be so far removed from the nature of human love that the concept is not at all reassuring.

Since I am not a theological scholar, I am going to stick to a personal, everyday religious viewpoint which has the advantage, I hope, of a greater degree of relevance to the everyday impact of religion than a more erudite approach. I suppose I am rather well placed to talk about morality, not because I am by any means virtuous—in fact quite the reverse, as I have always found it hard to stick to the rules—but chiefly because I have spent a fair amount of my professional time working in Hades with those who have been labelled bad, perverse, or dangerous, and often mad as well. I suppose the most consistent features to have emerged in my years of practice are the universal belief in personal goodness amongst those who have behaved badly and the conservative nature of the mind. It is extremely difficult to change patterns of behaviour, and, however shamed, vilified, or punished, the guilty hang on to their sense of goodness as they hang on to their sanity.

In many psychoanalytic models of the mind, sanity and a sense of goodness are closely connected; however, this has not always been the case, and Freud's original view of human nature was extremely gloomy. He saw the individual as harbouring a reservoir of unstructured, hedonistic drives that had to be repressed and modified by social pressure to conform to a more civilized way of behaving. (This idea is repeated often in Freud's writings but expressed most completely in *Three Essays on the Theory of Sexuality*, 1905d.) This is a common theme, particularly in fundamentalist religion where human nature is seen as savage, dangerous, and ungoverned. Piety is achieved through abstinence and celibacy. Desire is the path to evil and shuts one off from reaching truth and eternal beauty. Of course Freud was a mechanist and did not believe in the supernatural origins of man's instinctual difficulties, but there seems little doubt that he was influenced by this long superstitious attitude to passion as synonymous with the badness of human nature. Later, after the horrors of the First World War and impressed by the power of sado-masochism in human beings, he introduced his theory of the death instinct. This he saw as an innate tendency within the mind to return to a less complicated and highly energized system, reflecting the return of organisms to inorganic simplicity—a kind of psychic entropy.

Psychoanalytically, this tradition was modified, particularly in the United Kingdom, by the object-relations school of psychoanalysis, which, following Fairbairn, saw instinct as goal-directed and object-seeking so that a much more adaptive role was attributed to the inherent drives in human nature (see Fairbairn, 1952). In some ways this has been paralleled by religion, particularly in the Western world, where sin and the devil play a much less prominent part in ecclesiastical pronouncements. Priests have become steadily more pastoral to the point of being social workers or therapists rather than being driven by theological mysticism. In fact, more recent ideas have been advanced of God as an internal human drive to goodness in every individual, with expressions of disbelief in an external omnipotent God out there. The absolute divinity of Jesus Christ has been called into question by ecclesiastical thinkers such as Cupitt (1997), and this reflects the move away from supernaturalism in Western democratic societies.

As would be expected, many of the religiously enthusiastic are alarmed by this move and see, probably correctly, the decline of the devil as heralding the demise of real faith in God. In psychoanalysis, it was Klein who kept the flag flying as far as innate badness in human nature was concerned. Her concept of primitive envy as a manifestation of the death instinct is parallel to the notion of original sin (Klein, 1957). Indeed, her idea of a depressive position, in which an individual's innate ambivalence must be faced as a platform for the development of sanity, can produce, when it is addressed in treatment, something close to a religious conversion. Analysands are invited to face their primary envy, hatred, and destructiveness towards the "good object", and their sense of guilt at this point will be as intense as any penitent's visit to the confessional. Repentance then becomes part of the cure and, as such, must be allied with the parallel cures of religious conversion.

Both religion and psychoanalysis have plenty of material on which to support their interest in man's badness. To say that it is an innate aspect of being human or to preach original sin is another matter. My experience of the bad and the damned is that they almost always have a history of great suffering as children, if not of downright abuse, neglect, and violence. Sometimes one sees people whose badness appears to be unrelated to early experience, but often this turns out to be due to very early abuse of which the individual has no proper memory. Eventually, relatives may come forward who have seen some appalling act committed when the offender was a baby which no one has talked about let alone told the individual concerned. The idea that it was a good thing not to respond to infants when they cried for attention, which was fashionable between the wars and is beginning to creep back into child care in the philosophy of behaviourism, has done much to undermine the mental health and happiness of the offspring of anxious parents who suppressed their natural instincts on the advice of the experts in child-rearing. Whether one follows Klein or St Paul, if one is determined to establish that badness is innate then one would find ways of doing so whatever the misfortunes an individual may have suffered.

I remember well the seminar in which, as a psychoanalytic student, I listened to the reporting of a case by a fellow student in which an orphaned boy seeking treatment had brought an early dream.

He dreamt that *he found a cat damaged in the road and brought it home to look after it*. The student felt that this was a hopeful dream, suggesting that his patient wanted some help with a damaged part of himself. The seminar leader, however, an eminent Kleinian, dismissed this as pseudo-reparation, being herself quite certain that the damaged cat represented the damaged breast, the victim of the patient's innate envy, an envy that had prevented him from forgiving his neglectful mother and recovering from his years in the orphanage.

This anecdote illustrates, I think, the essential religious element in psychoanalysis. All analysts have beliefs that are irrefutable and, in order to try to illuminate their patient's material, must have faith in their special wisdom. The problem is that in operating this belief they may lose sight of the incredulity that should counterbalance the sanctity of dogma. A tendency to rebellion is perhaps the best bulwark against the mindlessness of piety. At least the psychoanalytic establishment will allow one to change one's mind without promising eternal damnation, and the tradition of independent thought in the British Psycho-Analytical Society is a good one. People get upset and may even talk of heresy. Moves may be made to make life difficult, but generally speaking original thought is encouraged even if it leads to battles. Indeed, Melanie Klein herself had a rough passage to establish her school of thought. These days, one of her theories, called projective identification, has become so popular that it is now used to explain both normal and abnormal mental processes. Often it is described as if it worked in some sort of supernatural way, transferring thoughts and mental matter from one mind to another and conferring special powers of perception on those who utilize the concept in their analytical work, heralding a temptation for them to believe that they have special access to the truth.

There is another comparison between psychoanalysis and religion in this question of good and bad behaviour, since both offer a method that is held to produce a change for the better. It has become extremely popular in recent years for politicians to support enthusiastically the idea that bad behaviour can be rectified by a combination of punishment and religious education, particularly in schools. I am afraid I have some depressing news for these moral optimists. The fact of the matter is that the capacity and inclination to behave well is acquired very early in life and will tend to run a natural course, however unpleasant the outcome and however pious the preaching. If one studies the personality features of those who are persistently antisocial, one can distinguish a fundamental psychological problem that differentiates them from those who behave better. This can be properly described as a problem of mental health. An important feature of mental health is the ability to buffer emotional stress. (I discuss this model of mental homeostasis in "The Psychopathology of Neurosis and Offending": Gallwey, 1990.) Vital internal relationships, on which the sense of safety of the self depends, need to be protected from the emotional reactions that would disrupt them, leading to excessive anxiety, a loss of mental equilibrium, and fears of mental disintegration.

In order to do this, the mind, from a very early age, develops the facility for a type of imagination that alters the impact of destabilizing experiences by fabricating a different version of the truth. This mental system of fabrication, which I have called *psychosynthesis*, is restrained by an opposite tendency to hang on to fundamental biological truths. (This use of the term *psychosynthesis* is different from that employed by Roberto Assagioli, 1975.) These truths are connected with the nature of our biological reality, in particular those of our historical dependence on the mother from conception through nurturing to a viable independence. I have called this tendency *psychopoesis*. The balance between these two tendencies, to falsify on the one hand and to hang on to truth on the other, has in mental health an extremely creative outcome. It is responsible for the flexibility and complexity of thought as well as the amazing achievements of the human mind in art, science, and philosophy. In a less grand way, this dynamic balance gives our everyday experiences a highly personal meaning that is specific to our own vulnerabilities and strengths, deriving from the uniqueness of our genetic endowment and the uniqueness of our fundamental experiences. If the need to buffer stress is excessive, then psychosynthetic alteration of reality becomes so omnipotent that the biological truths of dependency are lost and the outcome is mental illness. If this capacity is deficient, then maladaption and socially harmful behaviour result.

The development of a repertoire of imaginative strategies derives from the flexibility, affection, and relevance of the responses of the parents to the needs of their infant. Those who have had very adverse experiences of neglectful or cruel parents not only carry an identification with the bad parents, but their acquisition of a psychosynthetic capacity is impaired. Such individuals are already stressed by the social alienation they have acquired from their faulty nurturing and, in addition, are unable to amend the

impact of ordinary everyday stress by adjusting reality in imagination. As a result, they attempt to adjust reality itself, as if con-
structing a dream by utilizing objects in the external world. This
is often achieved in cruel, invasive, or violent attacks on others
that embody the essence of the perpetrators own historical experiences. I have discussed this more fully elsewhere (Gallwey, 1991).
If I am right, and I believe I am, then this deficiency accounts
for the intractability of bad behaviour and makes it impervious
to moral persuasion or coercion. It also renders punishment futile,
since punishment inevitably introduces, by its very nature, a
mental stress that most delinquents can only manage by resorting
to further delinquent behaviour. Prisons are hothouses that breed
delinquent strategies and so encourage the very thing they are
supposed to subdue.

It may very well be thought that in this last account of badness I have displayed a good deal of religious thinking. In common with most psychoanalytic models of the mind, my theory,
although derived from study and observation of the personalities
to whom I am applying it, can nevertheless not be subject to strict
scientific examination of the kind that those who follow Karl Popper's definition of science would demand. Since psychoanalysis
cannot fulfil this definition, some have argued that it is the same
as a religious belief.

The methods of physics and chemistry rely on the possibility of
strict refutability of hypothesis. This in turn relies upon strictly
defined entities that can be shown to be either right or wrong. As
has been described, the mental impact of reality is experienced in
an artistic manner as a product of psychosynthetic and psycho-
poetic functions. Hence, most mental events are neither true nor
false but something in-between that is essentially fluid, each event
merging with, changing, and being changed by those in association with it. The primary object of dependency and the primary
sense of self are the two fixed points of reference that are known
instinctually and provide, together with the primary linking functions, access to systems of logical inference when the capacity for
abstract thinking is achieved. The meaning of this activity is the
affirmation of the primary duality of ourselves in a dependent
relationship with a mother. (A common mistake in argument,

which can lead to much heat or even violence, is to confuse the psychological satisfaction of making a valid inference with the logical significance of the inference per se. See Bertrand Russell, 1919, p. 149, on truth value.) The terms of this ultimate equation are unalterable, as is the function between them—that is, I was loved, therefore I am; I need love, therefore I think. It is my belief that I can detect in the analysis of mental disturbance the origins of thought disorder. Since everyone's personal identity was achieved in infancy through primary functions of attachment from which the origins of the logical connectives can be understood to have derived, then malfunction of these connectives indicates the nature of the disturbance in infantile bonding experiences. (I have endeavoured to describe how this can be demonstrated in psychoanalytic practice in "Psychotic and Borderline Processes": Gallwey, 1996.) The beauty of achieving a mathematical proof lies in the successful rediscovery of coherence when the confusion of very complex relationships between abstract entities is finally resolved, like finding one's way home through a highly dangerous maze.

The best way to study someone else's mental life is to use one's own mental state for doing so, which is what psychoanalysis attempts under especially controlled conditions. These conditions involve the suspension of the analyst's needs as far as possible, including the need to moralize, reassure, or give advice. The analyst actively attempts to confine responses to understanding the needs of the patient as they emerge in the sessions. The purely mental experience of the relationship with the patient is used systematically in an attempt to illuminate the nature of his experiences of his self in life. The therapeutic element rests upon the belief that from this controlled relationship the patient can find a different meaning in his life which is closer to the truth of his existence and that this will be helpful. It is a difficult and somewhat arrogant undertaking, and, like religion, it is concerned with fundamental truths. These are not, however, God-given but biologically-given. Once psychoanalysis, as it often does, strays in its fundamental axioms from what is biologically the case, then it becomes over-abstract and fanciful. There is a tendency in psychoanalytic discourse to cover up ignorance by elaborate inventiveness, and this has done much to discredit the discipline as something to be taken seriously. However, when properly restrained, psychoanalysis gives access to the extraordinary capacity of human beings for an entirely individual phantasy life, containing amazing versions of life events and an instinctual knowledge of fundamental biological realities.

The most important of these realities is our dependence on others, a dependency that at its inception is the most prolonged of all biological creatures and is experienced in health as a feeling of love and the protectiveness of others. In my view, the infant is born with a knowledge of itself as an entity but needs the affirmation of good mothering to fully discover itself and its own innate potential. In this formulation, the discovery of the self goes hand in hand with the discovery of a loving protective other. This dual discovery of a self dependent upon a dependable other is the basic primary identification, which I have called the *vital concept*. In the vital concept, separateness and individuality are affirmed within the context of a loving dependency, and it remains throughout life as a platform for emotional development and the template of identity. The combination of separateness and dependency heralds an independence based on interdependency, which is the essence of morality and social coherence. Society and the various cultures within it hang together by the operation of mutual interdependence of varying kinds, from love relationships to the invisible fields of inter-reliance that constitute the fabric of any culture. Through these, there is a constant affirmation and re-affirmation of the vital concept. The experience of goodness, beauty, and truth in the world derives from the re-discovery and re-affirmation of the vital concept, with its deeply biological and species-specific characteristics. Contrariwise, badness, cruelty, and deceit derive from obliviousness, neglect, or attacks upon the vital concept or its social equivalents.

Here is the humanist moral standard against which the morality of an action, or even a thought, can be measured. It is not utilitarian or altruistic. It certainly does not depend upon the worship of a God or obedience to any external authority. It is highly adaptable to different circumstances, and the actions that spring from it are never infallible or perfect but can be considered as the best that can be expected for any individual under the circumstances prevailing. It is not strictly utilitarian and avoids estimates of happiness of a kind proposed by Jeremy Bentham or desirability as proposed by John Locke. In fact, being true to the vital concept may bring unhappiness and hardship, even appalling suffering. It is the measure of the strength of the contact with the vital concept which enables extraordinary feats of human bravery, just as the appalling inhumanities of humans towards each other is a reflection that it has been lost.

How does this approach compare with that of religion? Religion seems to me to detach the importance of the vital concept, particularly the concept of the dependable other, by transposing it into a supernatural being almost invariably with a masculine identity. The beauty of the dependency on the parents, so central to the vital concept, is dehumanized into absolute obedience to this almighty being who is given supposedly infinite powers of creation, knowledge, and control. Sets of rules, held to have derived from this almighty being but brought to us generally by his prophet with the assistance of a priesthood, are then used as the moral absolutes against which our actions will be judged. Once one has stepped outside religious belief, it becomes in many ways extremely puzzling as to why anyone should believe, let alone obey, this kind of authoritarian mythology.

The idea of a Father in heaven, omnipotently looking after us, was described by Freud as patently infantile and has been challenged by many thinkers, notably David Hume who claimed that the existence of evil was incompatible with the concept of an omnipotent and morally perfect god. Logical analysis of God's apparent neglect of the world (in terms of the innocent suffering natural disaster and appalling cruelty) and philosophical arguments such as those of P. J. McGrath (1995) have, it seems to me, only limited appeal. It is, after all, the mystery and power of God that is stressed as much as his goodness. If this is accepted as beyond questioning, then one can only say, as did Kierkegaard, that His love is completely beyond human understanding. Kierkegaard (1843) used the story of God's command to Abraham to kill Isaac, his only son, to argue that no human being could put anyone through such an experience in the name of love, since it involves such mental torture, even if in the end he was not asked to carry it out. The worst form of inhumanity practised by tyrannies is to make the victims watch their infants or children being tortured, so Kierkegaard's argument is powerfully made. He concludes that the reality of God's love cannot be comprehended by human beings, and that we can only live in fear and trembling beneath the yoke of such a terrible and incomprehensible love— not knowing at any moment what may be our fate. It is often the case that however unjustified the suffering, however innocent the victims, the faithful will cling to belief in a benevolent God.

Many people's faith in a benign God springs largely from a sense of safety in the world, often accompanied by wonderment in the combination of order and complexity in the scheme of things, giving for them a sense of communication with the Almighty. In my view, these experiences derive from a successfully achieved vital concept and are very much part of mental health. In daily life, the sense of safety is somewhat unwarranted and is readily shattered when life-threatening stress overwhelms the buffering capacity of the mind. The sense of safety is then replaced by a perpetual sense of vigilance, with states of panic at any reminder of the stress. Without such extremes of experience, our existential security is not eroded by those things that more neurotic individuals find constantly frightening, such as the danger of criminal attacks, the unpredictability of disease, unsignalled harm to loved ones, or any other event that makes our existence much less sound than this sense of safety persuades. It would not be possible to carry on if we were to consider every danger that might be around the next corner or, indeed, every sin that we might at any moment be committing. There are individuals who are paralysed by such doubts having only to hear that a meteorite may collide with earth to live in terror that they will be the sudden victim of annihilation, or who, in noticing a passing sexual thought, become convinced of a terrible damnation of their souls.

It seems to me that belief in a benign God is the expression in mystical terms of the sense of existential safety derived from the knowledge of the nature or the genesis of the self within the context of healthy sexuality and loving nurturing. Biologically and psychologically, this sense of safety springs largely from the mother, for it is she who generates the life that one enjoys and does the major share of the early linking functions. This is a blow to male grandiosity, which, in order to hang on to cultural dominance, produces gods who are masculine and a masculine priesthood to pursue the suppression of others, particularly women, within the sanction of mystical dogma. The fear of sexuality and the control of women, as well as their subordination, are central themes of religion, from Hinduism to Christianity. The flight from fear and weakness into grandiosity, particularly by men, has been the mainstay of religious tyrannies through the ages and remains so in many cultures.

It is the institutionalization of religion which results in these abuses, for institutions become easily self-serving to a growing sense of self importance, thereby losing track of their dependent social function. Religious groups are already embarked on this track, believing as they do that they have a hot-line to infallibility. Many people in these groups use the mythology of their belief as a personal badge of superiority, and this narcissistic element blends invisibly into the more grandiose tyrannical abuses with which the faithful in all religions so easily become involved.

Psychoanalytic institutions have been compared to priesthoods, and the essentially artistic core of the discipline gives those who practice it a tendency to omniscience so that psychoanalytic institutional status often deteriorates into moral certitude.

Many Jewish analysts, perhaps the majority, have their boy infants circumcised. I remember describing the misery of a Jewish patient of mine who had watched horrified as her child was taken from her arms by a mumbling mystic and brought back to her bleeding and distraught. She was subsequently racked with a good deal of self-doubt about the legitimacy of abandoning her infant to such a pointless and bloody ritual. The occasion when I raised this was a symposium on violence, in which the cultural relativism of human cruelty was being advanced by the sociologists. However, it was not the sociologists who got upset with me, but a Jewish analyst who suggested that my patient's distress at the circumcision of her infant was indication of her unresolved psychopathology rather than distressed maternal love. It was one of the many occasions in my psychoanalytic career when I felt an upsurge of doubt in a discipline in which the identification of pathology depended so much upon the analyst's prejudice, so unlike the clearer methodology enjoyed by the experimental sciences.

It is surely important to understand why beliefs in all-powerful, highly punitive almighty beings have been such a prominent part of human history. It is manifestly the case that the decay in the power of the church and the decline in religious practice has brought a steady increase in the freedom of the individual and protection from the worst excesses of the state within Western democracies. Up until recent times, the church tended to oppose all movements towards greater freedom, was opposed to the liberation of women, and sanctioned cruelty and exploitation of children as an extension of God's authority through the parents and the state. In considering this question, it is necessary to make a distinction between religion as a set of mystical beliefs supported by a priesthood and the social practices that the priesthood enforces by reference to the scriptures.

Most religions are such a complicated set of axioms and recommendations that it is possible to support almost any course of behaviour as morally necessary or morally condemnatory by finding some appropriate quotation from the relevant book of words. Russell, in his 1930 essay on religion's contribution to civilization, quotes Matthew (10: 35–37) to demonstrate that Christ appears to have had somewhat destructive thoughts about filial affection within the family. Kierkegaard (1843), likewise in support of the absolute duty to God, quotes Luke (14: 26) "If any man come to me and hate not his father, and mother, and wife, and children, and brethren and sisters, yea, and his own life also, he cannot be my disciple." Kierkegaard remarks that "this is a very hard saying, who can bear to hear it? For this reason it is not heard very often." It is certain that those who invoke Jesus Christ in their support for family values and the authority of the parents will avoid these particular passages in the scriptures. Russell also points out that the Christian Church, both Protestant and Catholic, shows no intention whatsoever of following some of the recommendations of Jesus Christ: to give away worldly goods to the poor, not to fight, not to judge others, not to punish adultery. The moral directives of religious doctrine, which are supposed to form the ideal from which we derive our morality and without which we are told we would have none, are largely expressions of the awful power of the Almighty and the command to be obedient to Him. The ten commandments are essentially about this obedience. The ones about not stealing, killing, or coveting are not only not practised but, like killing, become morally mandatory in wartime or, like coveting, are the driving force of a free-market economy. I suppose that adultery is the only one that is inescapably central to good behaviour, provided that one means by adultery not simply the breaking of marriage vows, but the betrayal of personal gratitude and loyalty to the vital concept and to those who most exquisitely represent it in one's contemporary life.

What is true of Christianity is also, as far as I can gather, equally true of other religions such as Islam. The greatest sin, as with Christianity, is blasphemy or breaking God's word, and the punishments are just as dreadful. What actually constitutes breaking God's word and how the punishments are to be delivered is another matter, one that depends on the social situation in which the believer is operating and the nature of the political power the priesthood are wanting to operate.

The worst excesses of genocide and the abuse of human rights have been perpetrated by atheistic tyrannies of communism and fascism. Nevertheless, there is a very clear equivalence between those done in the name of some God through the secular institutions of the particular religion and the excessive barbarity of the totalitarian atheistic states. (For a discussion of the former phenomenon, see *Islamic Terrorism?*, Ahmad, 1989.) They all have the characteristic of excessive cruelty and infallible authoritarian paternalism in which there is an attempt to control, through fear and repression, not only the way individuals behave but the very things they think. If one takes the vital concept as the measure of human goodness, then the history of religion through the church, by and large, has been the most profound attack upon natural morality itself.

The increasing freedom of the individual since the Enlightenment has been accompanied not only by a decline in the power of the state, but a decline in the extent to which religion and the church have directly influenced the state and sanctioned its atrocities. The freedom of the individual is inversely proportional to the power of the church, and it seems entirely contradictory that there should be so much recommendation for a return to the latter.

The essence of the problem lies in the tendency for men to move towards a hatred of the vital concept when their dependency needs are threatened. Under these conditions, men find it much more difficult than women to maintain contact with the primary internal relationship in which the status of infantile dependency and the importance of the mother go hand in hand, and they more readily resort to attempts in phantasy to dominate the internal maternal object. Female infants are able from early on to compensate for deficiencies in the quality of their attachment to the mother. They have a very efficient form of psychosynthesis to hand by turning their innate knowledge of their own potential maternalism and sexuality into a pretend realization that they have achieved it. This makes their bodies the concrete equivalent of the vital concept. Socially, this normal self idealization is realized by corporal decorations, display, or hiding.

Display is much more popular with the churches, and it is no accident that the male priesthood in nearly all religions enjoy showmanship and personal adornment of their bodies. There is always something unconvincing, however, about the male transvestite, whether on the musical stage or performing in front of the altar. Men have much further to go before they can establish a belief in themselves as ideal representatives of the maternal aspect of the vital concept. On the positive side, this deficit in psychosynthetic capacity drives men to compete creatively with the primary dependable object by excelling in social activity, whether that be intellectual, artistic, or practical. These endeavours often contain an appreciation internally of the vital concept and, for this reason, are socially creative. However, when the strains maintaining contact are too great, then there is a flight into omnipotence, grandiosity, and paranoid superiority. Masculinity and paternalism become inflated and idealized; contact with the vital concept is lost. Obedience to this megalomaniac authority is demanded particularly of women and children. Such inflated men hate the child in themselves as much as the object on which that child depended for its survival. Their self-righteousness is only matched by their appetite for punishment and the control of others. Often lip service is paid to women and to motherhood. This pseudo-affection is surrounded with prohibitions towards sexual freedom and individual choice so that women and children are only tolerated essentially as slaves, with a gloss of sentimentality to hide the repressive reality.

This situation is not exactly the fault of the religion as a purely mythological device. The situation is driven by the need for particular men to seek positions of power through the priesthood. An alliance then develops between the priests and the state authorities. These are powerful reasons for the separation of church and state, and a powerful reason to check the power of the state through democratic open government, as Karl Popper advances in his political writings. (Popper draws an interesting parallel between scientific refutability and democratic freedom.) Let us hope that the feminists see the real point of their ascent to authority and do not allow a chance for a new kind of social creativity to be undermined by those who are mainly motivated by their hatred of men. These unfortunates will inevitably aspire to a controlling grandiosity and mimic the paternalistic tyrannies they have striven to supplant, and they need to be vigorously resisted.

Psychoanalysis has no such aspirations to control or dominate. (Foucault and Szasz would disagree with this proposition.) It aims, *inter alia*, through the amelioration of harsh aspects of the vital concept and the deflation of grandiosity of the self, to set the individual free from fear of authority or an appetite for power. It is the case that Freud showed a distinctly diminished view of women and an overemphasis on the role of the father. Female analysts, especially Melanie Klein, have adjusted this so that not only has the central role of the feeding mother been explored but the drive to grandiosity made accessible through the description of early psychotic mechanisms.

Because psychoanalysis and the therapies that properly derive from it attempt to help their patients face the reality of death, I want to end by saying a word or two about immortality.

As I have indicated, the vital concept is the ability of humans to be aware of their biological realities. It is inescapably the case that we were conceived by a sexual event, that we grew in our mothers' bodies, and that the affirmation of ourselves depends upon the good fortune of having a good-enough mother. The other inescapable reality is that we will die and that, whatever happens in between our birth and our death, we are not going to get a second chance for fulfilment. The extraordinary difficulty in grasping non-existence and the terror of premature annihilation makes death an extremely difficult reality to grasp. Quite ordinary, pleasant people—including some very intelligent individuals—believe in immortal life, often as a prize for good behaviour, and fail to grasp what a meaningless concept this is. It seems quite natural that people could find the idea of death very hard to face, but the persistence of belief in an afterlife is extraordinarily durable. It is something in which there seems little social harm because it seems so understandable. However, I am going to argue that it does insidiously undermine the fullness of experience in various ways.

In my model of the development of human sanity, conceptualization of the self as an independent entity is achieved through the dependent relationship with a mother and father and is crucial to the genesis of thought. Thought springs from the awareness of a gap in time and space between the self and the objects of need, as well as a perception of differences in ability and function. These psychological gaps are filled with mental events (phantasies and inchoate thoughts) that act as a bridge between self and other. Time and space, therefore, form an essential frame in which meaning is discovered. Ultimately, all this springs from a human's ability to achieve through an instinctual partnership with the parents, especially the mother, self-conscious access to the fundamental biological realities of the self.

One of these realities is that life is finite, that we have a potential to be realized when we are born, and that death is inevitable. In fact, all meaning has a temporal and spatial dimension, and giving meaning to experience is the central feature of human consciousness. The idea of an eternal life is not only unlikely but meaningless. You might not want to relinquish beauty, excitement, and the brilliance of experience, but it is only its finiteness that makes it so brilliant. It is only the knowledge of termination which allows the beauty of objects to be manifest, and nothing that lasted forever could have any significance at all in human understanding. Infinity cannot be imagined and only has meaning as a mathematical function. The infinitesimal span of time and the relative minuteness of the pocket of space in which we live makes the immensity of the universe not only a source of awe in terms of itself, but, precisely because we make measurements in time and space when considering its reality, its immensity increases the significance of our life within it. What a precious thing to be alive amongst all that vast swirling dead matter without which we would not exist. What an incentive to love life and make the most of it before we become a literal part of its silent disintegration.

It is difficult to imagine one's disappearance, and so we tend to think of death as a state of affairs rather than simply the disappearance of the self. Because we learn something of the past before we were born, we get the illusion of having been around long before we actually arrived. It is a different matter to imagine vacating the neighbourhood of one's present existence and to have no future. Yet if the stone wall of death can be faced, then the very uniqueness and finiteness of our experiences, although they may be a minutely small element in the totality of things, gives them an enormous meaning.

I find this enormity, and the thought of it ending for good, at times too overwhelming—but not so unmanageably that I would grasp at the offer of an almighty God. Those who have suffered great loneliness and isolation, not knowing whether they were going to live or die—those, for instance, who have been held hostage—describe how they cling to the memory of their loved ones to see them through. I have noticed the same with prisoners. It is to the visit, the letters from their wives and girlfriends, the memory of their children that all except the extremely perverse turn to see them through. There is of course occasionally talk of God or Jesus, but by and large all turn to memories of human love to help them through loneliness, the threat of death, and the management of pain.

When someone dies, it is hard to come to terms with the fact that they have gone for good, to find an honest appraisal of one's feelings about them, and to take a measure of the meaning of the loss. Religious talk of them still being alive somewhere, of existing in some heaven with the possibility of reunion, detracts from the achievement of mourning and the appreciation of what one has lost.

I was at the funeral of a friend not so long ago, a young man who had left a family behind him, killed suddenly in a tragic accident when working on the maintenance of a North Sea oil rig. The church was packed, for he was a popular man, as is his family, full of life, bravery, and energy, with no little element of gallantry about him. For some time, the congregation emitted that numbed vacuousness and mindless obedience to ceremony that is the hallmark of Anglican worship. Not a tear was shed as far as I could see, but a kind of paralysed misery pervaded the church. The priest tried to persuade us that our dead friend was, even now, with God and that we would all meet again through the love of the Almighty and his son, Jesus Christ. We were told that we could now understand how Peter must have felt when he saw the body of Christ. There was in this no little hint that the crucifixion and death of Jesus Christ was a much greater tragedy than the death of our friend. I was unable to perceive that this approach did much to help people manage or appreciate what had happened now that our friend had been annihilated.

Happily, the deceased's mother came to the rescue. She had clearly become impatient with the way that the event was being hijacked by the clergy and, rising to her feet, announced that she was going to say a few words about her son. What she told us were simple stories of his boyhood, of his growing and his maturity, stories that enhanced his reality and showed us how much more there was to know of him. The effect on the congregation was immediate. The sound of grief swelled out more movingly than any congregational prayer or solemn music; at once his life was real and his death was real. The religious myths, the priesthood, and the rituals were suddenly redundant, and we all took the first step into mourning and an appreciation of what we had lost.

It seems to me the attack on truth and reality represented by religious belief is insidiously undermining, and I find myself increasingly objecting to the imposition of the Christian myths on my children when they are at school. Fortunately, they have developed a healthy scepticism, a love of life, and a high regard for others, all of which, I hope, springs from their parents' encouragement to be themselves, to be free in thought and opinion, and to hold that as more important than obedience or respect of authority. They are remarkably truthful, they behave well, and they are loving. They do not believe in God and feel no need for psychoanalysis. I would have liked to have had that advantage.

CHAPTER SIX

Reflections
of an analytical psychologist
on God, religion, and spirituality

Judith Hubback

Background and beginnings

Becoming an analytical psychologist, as I did in the 1960s, involved training along the ways of thought, study, theory, and experience which had evolved from Jung's work earlier in the century. One reason why I chose that training, rather than the one on offer at the Freudian Institute of Psycho-Analysis, was that I knew, in a vague way, that Jung had not agreed with Freud's view that being religious was a form of neuroticism, and that he had studied many aspects of religion very fully. I did not see myself as religious, but I knew that the subject mattered to me. The Jungian programme of professional training at that time, where the study of theory is concerned, was much less stringent than it became later. It was to my liking in being undogmatic. At first, like most trainees, I found Jung's writings difficult, as his style is associative rather than logical. But his learnedness appealed to me, and we were not expected to be disciples or believers, or to venerate all that he had ever written as in some way gospel truth. His struggles over what he discovered about every aspect of the human mind, of which man's relation to God or to the image of God was an important factor, his ambivalences and contradictions were distinctly appealing. In the mid-twentieth century, an age of major uncertainties when the "Leader" had become a dirty word, I did not want a role-model who had solved all problems satisfactorily and reached undeniable conclusions. When asked in 1959 by John Freeman in the BBC "Face to Face" interview whether he believed in God, Jung answered that he did not need to believe: he *knew*. That sounded self-satisfied and shockingly categorical. What it meant was that he went by his own subjective experience of God since what is generally called God is really the inner image of God. But of course he knew that many people see God as an objective fact, a transcendent Being.

As Jung was born in 1875, he was of the same generation as my father, born five years earlier. I see myself as descended, on the male side, from two men who had some personal similarities although their lives developed along very different professional lines. They both had powerful minds and were basically serious men, conscientious and thorough to a fault, deeply committed to what they could contribute to the people with whom they had chosen to work. Both their personalities were many-sided, but Jung can be described as the more earthy of the two; he enjoyed working with his hands, but more than that he was easily spontaneous and could be openly angry. My father was chiefly very clear-thinking; his father had been a successful businessman, conventional for his time and class, probably uncommunicative to his academic son, whereas Jung's father was an anxiety-ridden pastor which affected Jung deeply. Though Jung's mother was psychologically very influential, she was physically often absent owing to illness, whereas my father's mother died when he was a small baby so the effects of the trauma were presumably more hidden. Jung integrated the various features of his psychological and religious inheritance, achieved his own way of being himself, and left a huge legacy to probably millions of troubled souls. In contrast, my father did not appear to have shaken off the inhibitions on emotion with which he grew up; however, he developed, with many friends, his strong intellectual energy fully and used it on behalf of international relations, about which he had strong feelings. He relied on a basically ethical attitude to life which was fed by an underground water-table of spiritual values. In the copy of the Bible which he gave me, he inscribed the words of the prophet Micah: "What doth the Lord require of thee, but to do justly, to love mercy, and to walk humbly with thy God?" My reaction to that, at the time, was a sense of its severity; it reined-in the risk of displaying embarrassing emotions. Late in life, I can now feel the value of it. Another view of the Lord might include permission to find a smile, even if only a small and rueful one.

Where the thinking function is concerned, I am fortunate to have had two such deep-minded fathers, although the effect of them conveying to me that I also should push myself to the uttermost in strenuous ways of life has often been an excessive burden. Inheriting more of the care-free, semi-flirtatious Edwardian youth of my artistic mother would have been valuable. But her Anglican High Church mother was also influential, because she had always conveyed that a lot of attention should be paid to serious matters such as religion and sexual morals. Conventional sexuality was assumed, never discussed. There were two major sins: being selfish (including being "swollen-headed") and telling a lie. The taboo on selfishness was, of course, necessary since (like all taboos) it was so likely to be infringed. There was no conception, within this high-minuends, of the ordinary child's need for her healthy narcissism to be acceptable. As any analyst can see, that left a legacy needing a lot of working on. It has even contributed to trouble in my being fully comfortable with the central theory of the self in analytical psychology and the part it plays in the approach to individuation which, put briefly, is the developmental process of integrating as many aspects of the personal psyche as possible, becoming ever more conscious of all one's nature and potential: one's self. The vestigial child in me still finds that inevitable *word* difficult, though the adult understands its meaning, at least approximately, and is certain it must be aimed at. Working towards it now includes, for me, a pressing concern to integrate spirituality with the material and practical aspects of life. Jesus' apparently simple recommendation to "love thy neighbour as thyself" fits in well with my experience of analysis and my professional career. And it is now my central belief that relating in its many forms is the core characteristic of both analysis and spirituality: relating with one's self to the self of the patient, and relating one's own self to an inner sense of God—the numinous power beyond matter, inspiring ultimate awe, the source and essence of all qualities, especially love. At times I regret that I find it difficult to fit in with any religious organization, with creeds and accepted rules, which also offers company. But I see the Spirit of God as paradoxically both inner and boundless. I realize that, in contrast, for many people God is to be found in a particular religion. And each religion has to ask for at least a minimum of conformity.

In my childhood, ethical considerations were self-evident, implicit, and conveyed rather than openly discussed. I now think that they were moralistic rather than simply ethical. That gave them, of course, a dangerous power. Conformism in the matter of church attendance was expected. There was much pained disapproval from my mother when, after I had experienced Confirmation as disappointingly empty of any emotion, I refused to keep on going to the Communion service. With hindsight, it was perhaps that I only saw the concreteness and missed out on the symbolism. It did not feed the part of my psyche which I now see was longing for something deeply important to help me make sense of what was going on in my inner world: what values could I live by? Hypocrisy and complacency had to be challenged. I thought that Pilate's question "What is truth?" was a valid one. What is real honesty? What is reliable? What about toleration? The history of many religions, and not only the Christian one, and of "religious" people torturing and massacring each other was far from reassuring, let alone inspiring.

At that stage, Shelley influenced me deeply, not only with his poetry but also with the tract that led to his expulsion from Oxford, *The Necessity of Atheism* (Shelley, 1811; 1915). It was blazingly youthful and defiant. He was attacking with simplistic intellectual tools the same hypocrisy in contemporary established religion as Blake also had done in his poetry. The person and the life of Jesus appealed to both of them: I saw myself as their disciple since what I thought of as nearly socialist early Christianity

was an acceptable manifestation of religion. Jesus was pre–
Church of England. In the more mature *Essay on Christianity*,
Shelley showed that he had absorbed the spirit and the ethics that
Jesus considered essential and was championing his views on social justice as well as what he, Shelley, described as his feeling
about God who was for him "the overruling Spirit of the collective energy of the moral and material world" (Shelley, 1815;
1915). That simple enthusiasm for the Spirit, typical of so much
of his poetry, was infectious. His energetic *Ode to the West Wind*,
in which he invoked the "Wild Spirit, which art moving everywhere, Destroyer and preserver; hear, oh, hear!", was one that I
was prone to shout inwardly. I was trying to stave off the complicated angers and ambivalences of depression: how much to keep,
how much to reject? What I think of as "the energy of the spirit"
is psychological, but it can lead to the development of what can
validly be called spirituality with its indefinable extra quality.

I doubt if Shelley's prose is much read today: its tone is un-
comfortably elated and its thinking is woolly. But when much
later I read Rudolph Otto's *The Idea of the Holy* (1923), which is
much more sophisticated than Shelley's *Essays*, I saw affinities
between the carefully dry theologian and the romantic young
poet, and the themes that their writings offer. The seeds of a sense
of spirituality were sown for me through studying Shelley and
many other poets, as well as enjoyment of natural beauty in the
country and by the sea. I had, at intervals, a few experiences that
had an inspiring non-material quality, and I think it would not be
right to denigrate them as merely adolescent. An intuitively recognized small taste of the holy, or the numinous in Otto's terms,
does not have to be magnificent to be valuable and to carry meaning, nor does such a person have to be out of the ordinary.
Numinous events are private and do not necessarily happen in
prestigious religious places or during pilgrimages. Saint Teresa of
Avila, who was, of course, far from ordinary and had sensation-
ally powerful mystical seizures, found that when she was writing
she had to make use of comparisons, metaphors and symbols
since her experiences could not be put into intelligible words. It is
that way even in the safety of analysis, where hints and indica-
tions are enough if the analyst is receptive. Strongly significant
sessions with several of my own analytic patients have had the

same kind of indescribable quality, though I am not saying they were fully spiritual. There can be something ineffable sensed as being "of the spirit", between two people, when words would be like ruining the bloom on a plum with even gentle handling.

The years leading to analysis: the overlapping of attitudes

Those are some of the influential background factors that led me to attempting this chapter, and, in the course of writing it, I have found that the past and the present have had to be described in a closely interwoven way. From the angle of clarifying my views on what I think are the three themes of this book—God, ourselves, our work—the fact that my university years were those of the approach to the Second World War is a crucial one. The Italians under Mussolini, the begetter of Fascism, invaded Abyssinia on the day I arrived in Cambridge. History was my degree course; I was interested in international affairs and liberalism in the broadest sense. There was war in the Far East; the Nazis were gaining ground all the time, spreading the poison of murderous anti-Semitism, and subjugating the minds of countless people in central Europe. The Spanish Civil War seemed to me and my like-minded friends to clinch the inherent antagonism between the more or less democratic forces we admired and the terribly dangerous dictatorships. In our anxiety, we saw "good" and "bad" as sharply contrasted. That simplistic view could not last, and later I found Jung criticizing the equivalently crude attitude of "either/or".

From the distance of many years, it is now obvious that we chose to ignore much that we did really know, and dividing the "good" regimes from the "bad" ones was naive to a degree that it is now painful for me to remember. But the main mistake came from believing that, because the Soviet Union championed the United Front against Fascist Italy and Nazi Germany, it seemed right to believe that we should work with the Soviets. The great disillusion happened when Stalin cynically aligned himself with Hitler in August 1939. Idealism died a quick death, blinkered illusions that had been held too long gave way to heart-sinking fears

88   JUDITH HUBBACK

since it was immediately obvious that the lives (bodies and psyches) of millions of ordinary people were at risk. I was beginning
to see that the various forms taken by the defence of denying
(fending off, postponing, pretending, making excuses etc.) were
very dangerous.

The connection between how I saw the effects on individuals
of absolutist power-politicians and the very different essence of
the analyst–patient interaction, which I did not discover until
about twenty years later, is an obvious one: the analytical psychologist does not *tell* the patient what to do or think or believe,
dictating from a position of superiority on a "Jung said . . . " basis.
In the religious field, God as an inner spirit is different from the
God in any religion in which there is a definite creed based on
scriptures declared to be the words of God, even if that religion is
not a fundamentalist one. In analysis as well as in religion, politics, and the upbringing of children, there has to be respect for the
spirit as it lives in each person, provided that respect is granted to
others as maturing progresses.

Analysis

During analysis, I experienced my analyst accompanying me
through stressful difficulties, small recoveries, despairs and im-
provements. I realized how working from the inside to increase
the scope of consciousness was the essence of the matter in hand,
which I had only known theoretically before. It was the actuality
of basic respect; it had a fundamental and lasting influence. Ena-
bling the patient to develop through his or her times of inappropriate decisions, regressions and agonies is a different job from
being even a benign medical doctor who has authority of an in-
formational and directive kind. Powerful "white coat-ism", essential in physical medicine as compared to the power that comes
from interpreting the individual's often strange communications
with the help of well-tested theories and models of the psyche,
has almost gone from the psychotherapeutic world. The old tru-
ism of the difference between trying to cure and activating the
healing capacity of the patient has been overworked for some

while now, but it is still worth mentioning. I can also remember an incident during the training seminars when I discovered that other trainees who were psychiatrists said that they were having to alter many of their previous attitudes to patients. I was envious of them, with their aura of importance, and I was amazed when one of them said that she was envious of my background in the arts and human studies. The medical approach is, of course, necessary in a psychotic crisis, but it can be insidious at other stages if insufficiently analysed remnants of unconscious omnipotence are still at work in the analyst. It has a different internal quality from the containing and holding that analysts aim to provide. I have in mind the analogy between the image of a God who is primarily one who gives orders and one who relates with his feeling function and offers empathy rather than injunctions to those needing help. Feeling and empathy are manifestations of relating.

I have described at some length the connections between how I experienced the world in my growing-up years and why I became an analytical psychologist. They were crucial links in the process by which I moved from studying history in libraries (people in the past), experienced and observed personal interactions (a form of practical psychology), did some sociological research into the lives of married women graduates (Hubback, 1957), and stepped forward into analytical psychology. I came to see that, for me, history had contained the major theme of conflict between groups of all kinds (clans, classes, political parties, countries etc.) and conflicts between individuals, such as statesmen and religious leaders. The sociology that I studied was also about conflict, between the needs of women and those of men; how could we develop equivalence rather than demand crude equality? That contained some projecting of my own internal struggles. The concentrated inner work of analysis became essential, with its firm attention to raising into consciousness projections and other defences against anxiety. I discovered, among many other things, that both the intellect and emotion are ineffective when they are used defensively. I had previously used rational defences against the religion of my upbringing because, as far as I was concerned, it had died. But analysis enabled me to move towards what is now a sense of the importance of spirituality.

Training

Analysis and the training did not, for me, lead to the loss of a previously strong faith in religion, as I understand psychoanalysis does for some people. I had lost it many years before, as described above. Rather, together they gave me the opportunity to attend slowly and indirectly to spiritual matters in among other aspects of the human psyche. I sensed in a general way (and at one stage I saw more clearly through a series of dreams) that there were parts of myself I had never known or which were out of reach but worth struggling towards. There were also issues bigger than my personal self. That state of mind is fairly usual among people choosing a Jungian rather than a Freudian analysis. I could no longer postpone facing the difficulties that the searches would involve.

As well as Jung's considerable experience as a psychiatrist, his wide cultural interests and knowledge of myths and history were obvious, but in the training they were elaborated only when there were clinical applications to be deduced or points of theory. There was no question of either openly or covertly influencing future members of the Society of Analytical Psychology to move in the direction that Jung had taken where cultural or religious matters were concerned unless they wanted to.

Since the early 1980s Jung's books and papers on religious subjects have been included in the training at the Society of Analytical Psychology in London, but they did not feature when I trained. I think that the then Director of Training left the various aspects of religion, and Jung's writings on it, to each of us as individuals to work on for ourselves—if we wanted to. I think also that the main ones available then were most likely read by many trainees, if they could find time: "A Psychological Approach to the Dogma of the Trinity", "Transformation Symbolism in the Mass", and "Answer to Job" (all in *Collected Works 11*, 1958). When Jung's (1963) account of his stressful psychological development, *Memories, Dreams, Reflections*, was being discussed in a seminar with Michael Fordham, Jung's researches into the psychology of early Christian Gnosticism emerged as an important part of his interest in the history of the exploration of the unconscious and the symbols that it throws up. His attitude of trusting to where his researches led him appealed strongly to me. Fordham himself had recently published three chapters in *The Objective Psyche* (1958) on religion as connected with analytical psychology, including an enterprising one on the psychology of the mystical sixteenth-century monk St John of the Cross. In that study, Fordham specified that he wanted to examine Jung's thinking on religion and mysticism in order to free him, if possible, from invariably being called "mystical" as a term of abuse. Fordham found that he could productively link what emerged from his study of St John with the work on very early infant development on which he had already embarked: there were both similarities and major differences.

It is clear, from reading what Jung wrote about God, that he considered that the psychologist must study the *image* of God and the *idea* of God: the question of who or what the Deity is should be in the province of the theologian. To illustrate how he did not see religious belief as a neurotic trait, numerous quotations can be offered, such as "Everything to do with religion, everything it is and asserts, touches the human soul so closely that psychology least of all can afford to overlook it" (Jung, 1958, para 172). Disregarding religion would mean that matters to do with the soul were unimportant, whereas he saw the soul as an intrinsic part of the psyche, though it is not easy to give a simple definition of "soul". About God, he wrote: "It would be a regrettable mistake if anybody should take my observations as a kind of proof of the existence of God. They prove only the existence of an archetypal God-image, which to my mind is the most we can assert about God psychologically" (para 102). On another occasion he wrote: "We moderns are faced with the necessity of rediscovering the life of the spirit: we must experience it anew ourselves" (Jung, 1961, para 780). His interest in psychological balance between all the aspects of the psyche, including the striving for wholeness, is illustrated in "The utterances of the heart—unlike those of the discriminating intellect—always relate to the whole" (Jung, 1977, para 9). If religious concerns are kept separate, the psyche is impoverished. I have given a few quotations from Jung's writings to try to convey the general attitude that, in my opinion, characterizes many or perhaps most analytical psychologists in the matter of religion as linked with clinical work. In the supervision I received for my training patients, it was a strong theme (among others) that these patients needed the analyst to pay particular attention to the healing of defensive splits, to enable them to bring together thinking and feeling, and to lead them towards individuation.

When Jung's views on instinct were being studied, the following emerged: "The spiritual principle does not . . . conflict with instinct as such but only with blind instinctuality. . . . The spiritual appears in the psyche as an instinct, indeed as a real passion . . . a specific and necessary form of instinctual power" (Jung, 1960, para 108). We learned that Jung's statements about instincts were not so categorical as Freud's, since he discerned more versions or manifestations of instinctual drives after he had broken away from the older man, the idealized mentor whose views he had at first accepted almost wholesale. He increasingly saw instincts as dynamic factors in several groups: hunger, sexuality, activity and reflection. To those he added a fifth: "The creative impulse as a psychic factor similar in nature to instinct." These are the kinds of attitude to integration and wholeness that Jungian analysis works towards.

In brief words, and without an extended discussion of Freud's and Jung's views of instincts, archetypes can be defined as psychological instincts, and Jung conveyed that an instinct for spirituality stems from that archetypal root. Like the oedipal complex, the archetype of spirituality is found at work in many cultures, evidenced throughout history and (where spirituality and religion are concerned) expressed in diverse rituals.

While the main thrust of Jung's psychology is still entirely valid, some of what he wrote on cultural and anthropological matters has been disproved by later and more specialist scholars: it lacks their precision and is often diffuse, discursive and too imaginative through his desire to get observations to fit with his ideas and theories. The central ones revolved round his view of human beings needing more than material satisfactions. Not really very revolutionary or original. But he took the trouble to do his own fieldwork in the only way he could. And even though he comes across as rather gullible and simplistic, as compared with how he sounds when describing his clinical work, most of it was also refreshing. It was not exactly water in a parched land, but a bit like that. Thinking about it all was important and had to be combined with feeling into it. Areas of new interest were opened up, and a major task was to find ways of connecting the daily listening with matters of soul and spirit. I cannot remember tackling at that stage the difficult old question of what is the soul. It was a situation in which "sufficient unto the day" was applicable.

The spirit of God for a working analytical psychologist today

Being an analyst is both subtle and complicated. All that is involved cannot be put into a small compass. The many elements of the analyst's psychological inheritance—inborn personality, professional training and life experience—all interact with the parallel factors in his or her patients. Also, the working analyst's practice contains many and diverse people, some of whom may be suffering from long-term disturbances, others in immediate crises. In the course of the average day, the analyst uses elements of himself or herself in both direct and indirect ways, calling implicitly on both conscious and unconscious layers of the psyche with their many gifts, skills and defects. The patients seen in the practice project and introject transference factors that are sometimes easily identified, whereas at other times transferences and countertransferences are elusive or shift so rapidly within the session that it can be difficult for the analyst to keep a reliable sense of self. In both the straightforward times (the "bread and butter sessions" as Frieda Fordham called them) and the difficult ones, the key to reasonably good-quality work is reliance, not only on knowledge but also on the well-integrated self and its broad spiritual contents. My view is that the analyst exerts a practised ability to put aside, with confidence, private troubles even when they are very pressing, knowing that being well-centred subserves the needs of the patient and that the self is there to be called upon. And the confidence required of analysing in that mode is based on being able to rely on the spirit. The strength and the flexibility of the spirit develop with use.

In the course of my practice, I can remember only one person who, before embarking on analysis with me, enquired anxiously whether, if my views on religion were negative, she would be at risk of losing her faith. I thought it better not to answer directly or to interpret her anxiety at once but to encourage her to describe her religious beliefs and feelings, what it all meant to her, and so on. At the end of the session, she did not renew her question. When I asked her recently about how it had been (she is no longer in analysis), she said that she remembers me saying something about trust. In fact, as her analysis took shape, she discovered that she could trust her commitment to internal honesty in relation to religion as that firmed up and matured. Her religious sense was generous and free from left-over narcissism. I felt throughout the work with her that I could trust her sense of herself, which included her spirituality. Another patient, a man in his 80s, pushed me very hard on what is death. He did not mind the process of dying (so he said) but was very disappointed in me for not being able to tell him what happens afterwards. It seemed as though he was still mourning the absence in his actual childhood and teenage years of a parent willing to attend to his questionings. One of the trainees whose work I have supervised had a patient who refused to start analysis without being assured that the analyst was a Christian. The answer was yes, and the matter never came up again.

I cannot say with any confidence whether any of my patients have ever detected my personal views on religious matters or been affected by my struggles, unclear ideas, or, more recently, increasing interest in spirituality. But I think that my gradually looking older enables those who also have retirement and ageing difficulties to discuss dying, death and God since, as one said recently, she could see I knew just what she was talking about.

Whether the term "the spirit" on its own or the more suggestive term "the spirit of God" is used probably does not matter very much, though the theoretical and theological implications are important. I do not personalize God and find that "the spirit" is a kind of conglomerate, summation, or synthesis of spirituality's many contents. Those contents are, I think, the following: relating both directly and with awe to the other person and to the mysterious "other"; respecting these two versions of other-than-oneself; recognizing non-materiality; looking for ultimately believable values and towards truth, from which the desirable virtues follow. Such a list sounds grand and idealistic, but there has to be something grand when we are considering what the spirit means. Also it does not come amiss to have ideals, as well as aims, while recognizing that they are unlikely ever to be reached.

The concept of individuation in the sense of as much integration as humanly possible of all the contents of the psyche, conscious and unconscious, admirable and regrettable, is one that comes near to being a good tool for evaluating how effectively the spirit has been at work in a person. Using the concept in that sense is one of the major contributions of analytical psychology, its theories and its practice, because it centres on achieving the best possible relating between the different parts of oneself. And, adding to what I said above, the psychological act of relating is the essential element of the spirit as it takes form in humans. Perhaps there could be a plausible view of the Spirit of God as being on its own ("One is one and all alone / And evermore shall be so", in the words of the old song *Green Grow the Rushes-O*), but seeing it that way would take us into the region of theories and beliefs about the origin of the universe, about the creation of our world, which do not apply in the clinical work of analysis, though they can have a place if one is trying to explore what modern cosmologists have to offer psychologists who are interested in creativity. For the more ordinary, daily purposes I think that the spirit is most helpfully seen as awe in the face of the essence of relatedness and its many subtleties. Respect, whether for the holy or for the other person, flows from that.

To elaborate on the theme of the spirit and relatedness and respect: my position at present, as an elderly analytical psychologist, is that the spirit in some ill-defined form is setting me (and others, of course) the challenging task of finding out how I see God in action. Incidentally, it is a convenient convention to use the term God when struggling with the question of what there is beyond humanity, unless one is a rationalist or full-blown materialist. For thousands of years it has been a major preoccupation of innumerable people to consider and reflect on several possibilities about the Deity. In this regard, I would say the following: a transcendent force having somehow an actual existence; a non-human power that makes, or attempts to make, personal contact; a projection of the positive and admirable contents of our psyches, our basic needs, but perhaps also our wishes and desires; or something that we cannot get nearer to naming than to call it the Spirit of God. There is also the unpopular view (which was Jung's) that the totality of God contains both good and evil. He came to that through studying the intensity of pain in the biblical Book of Job (Jung, 1958). An either/or approach to the question of what is meant by "God" is unhelpful and inappropriate; there is no categorical answer to it to suit everybody. I recognize that my list of possible views is not exhaustive. It can only be applicable, at least in the main and in this chapter, to the developed religions and the thoughts of spiritual people in the contemporary world.

It has often been pointed out that when people grow old and are self-evidently in the third or even the fourth stage of their lives, they are much more likely to pay attention to fundamental issues, such as that of God's nature, existence versus non-existence, the meaning of life and the question of death, than they did in their middle years. Those are very broad generalizations, and what presumably has significance is the increase in attention, interest, or concern. For those of us who were already interested earlier in questions of life and death, as I was, but not alone in that and not in a strictly speaking religious way or form, it is annoying to be told that in considering death one is being morbid, as I have been by people unaffected by analytical thinking. The point is that in any analytical practice there are most likely quite a number of patients (and not only the older ones) who have suffered bereavements, sudden deaths, long life-threatening illnesses of their own or people they are closely connected with. So as an analyst, as well as from the basis of my own life which has included several of those causes of sadness, I have of course partaken in their reactions to any of those traumas. That said, it is in fact the case that concern about spirit and about death, of a feeling or emotional kind and interest, which is more a matter of the intellect, have both become very important to me as I approach the next decade. Decimal milestones of time always feel meaningful. There are birthday celebrations (they contain unspoken elements of consolation and encouragement) organized by family and friends. But there are also funerals, and the mystery of death asserts itself in an insistent way. Books and reflective thoughts help, denial and other defences become increasingly un-suitable. To my mind, the "Third Age" is a useful modern term, and it has added in depth to what Jung wrote about the onset of the second half of life.

While thinking about the various stages of life, there is an important analytical observation to be made. In old age, even more forcefully than earlier, it is essential to keep in touch with the Inner Child. One of the things about the infant and child stages of life is that during them the person is moving towards what they will be next. So keeping in touch with the Inner Child is appropriate at all ages and does not have to be seen as being infantile or pathologically regressed but about developing. Once the child is at school, it may learn to say the Christian "Our Father" prayer or perhaps it hears that other children do. Even nowadays, in our multi-cultural society, an implicit image of an archetypal father-God is on offer in the collective psyche, and, if the home atmosphere is benign, it will approximate to an idealized version of that parent, at least for a few years. The early psychoanalytic view of God (in the Vienna of Freud's time) was that it was a projection of a father imago: the infant needs the father since it feels so defenceless against all sorts of external dangers and against its frightening inner fantasies. The first days of life are dangerous, and unconsciously it fears death. When it is older, it discovers death as an actuality. In analysis, through the projection of its aggressive–destructive energy either into the analyst in the transference or against the persecutory environment, the earliest fantasies can be detected with certainty whether they are interpreted reductively or in a symbolic-archetypal way. These days, much attention is given to fantasies of omnipotence as compared with defencelessness. Babies in the flesh can be little dictators, dominating the whole house, as well as needing protection. Nowadays it is, I think, the mother who is seen as the psychological as well as the actual protector who lays the foundation for her infant to develop later a potential sense of God, or at least of some kind of God, even if the father is very present. It is worth noting that, historically, mother Goddesses preceded male gods. Protection is given to the infant in the safe holding boundaries of arms and lap; the psychological structure and tone are those of relating, laid down in these earliest days. Then working through the archetypal oedipal complex will offer the child the possibility of developing later, religiously, in depth, detached from the personal parents, if it so wants.

The impact of object-relations theory has spread from its beginnings in clinical theory and practice into the area of reflecting on God and spirituality. My impression is that quite a few present-day analytical psychologists are viewing and understanding the psychological foundation of belief in God as intrinsically that of relating to a power beyond the personal self, with the mother–infant relationship as the prototype. There is a strong appreciation of the psychological value of a God, or God-like power, relating to and respecting us, as well as vice versa.

In conclusion, I think that spiritual questions are being attended to more openly than they used to be, and more honestly, by a variety of analysts as well as by people in those allied professions that used to be considered less prestigious; their clients mostly come from areas of society which full analysis does not reach directly. But I also think that the influence of depth psychologists is possibly less in this sceptical and materially hyper-informed age than it was a generation or so ago. The historical figures of Freud and Jung are frequently under attack, in books and in other subtle ways. On a less pessimistic note, each individuated and reasonably whole analyst who has worked over the years to integrate his or her conflicts of instinct, feeling and intellect, bringing them together with the help of spirituality, is of diffused value in the wide world as well as in the concentrated one of the consulting-room.

CHAPTER SEVEN

Reflections about God (Yehovah) and religion

Judith Issroff

> "... there is nowhere a human being who can answer you those questions and feelings which have a life of their own within their depths; for even the best men go astray with words, when these are to express something very gentle and almost unutterable."
>
> Rainer Maria Rilke, 16 July 1903

I am not a believing atheist but a firmly agnostic Jewess. By unreasoned experience I am a sense-believer in what is known as a "soul" (Hebrew has five levels of development embraced by this one English word). But in reincarnation of soul, as in the question of God, I am unable either to believe or to disbelieve.

Many people hanker after transcendent moments or spirituality, but is this equitable with religious experience? Is a moment like that of satori or enlightenment in Zen Buddhism necessarily one of spiritual awakening or an illumination? Belief, ritual and spiritual experience are the cornerstone of religion. But are belief and ritual necessary for spiritual experience? Does spiritual development necessarily follow from belief and ritual practice? I think not.

Deeply respectful of psychic reality, I accept whatever faith is sacred to whomsoever. Yet where is my own faith? In doubting? In seeking plausible hypotheses to help me think perhaps I understand?

Judaism without the affirmation of some version of the traditional biblical view of God, Torah (the Jewish Bible) and covenant is but a socially constructed ethnic religion. I deeply appreciate the rich tradition and millennia of thoughtful discourse that is my people's heritage and contribution to mankind, but I cannot accept the Torah as divine revelation any more than these, my thoughts, nor attribute any superordinate significance whatever to the existence of the Jewish people [or any other people]. Even if the *Shoah* (the Nazi Holocaust) had not devastated my people during my lifetime, become an overwhelmingly defining plague in my consciousness, a subject of unwilling preoccupation and study, however disbelieving and assimilated I am, my "Jewish" identity and links are taken for granted, secure and indispensable. Although I am a natural heretic, I have never wanted to be other than "Jewish". But I am a Jewess who has read voraciously about other religions and explored widely from my given (historically, not notably secure) base. I know of no other religion more conscious and self-conscious than Judaism.

What about psychoanalysis?

Psychoanalysis is concerned with everything in human thought, behaviour and experience—nothing less. Religion is important in all societies, not excluding—however much we may object to religion—the esoteric forms that often pervade scientific societies. My own questioning and doubting extends to the worlds of narrow scientism, to psychoanalytic dogmas and to conforming practice.

I am as deeply and essentially a psychoanalyst as I am a Jewess, yet often I find myself sceptical, wondering about the basis and validity of what I encounter in some psychoanalytic literature or dismayed by what seems to me unquestioning adherence to doctrine—particularly as I encountered that during my psycho-analytic training in London in the late 1960s. I am indebted to those who encouraged my refusal to be psychoanalytically indoc-trinated.

As an Independent–Middle Group trainee, I attended all semi-nars—Kleinian, Anna Freudian and those of my unorganized, anti-groupie seniors. The then-prevailing psychoanalytic ethos was generally a conformity-demanding atheism and anti-religious attitude—except vis-à-vis the particular believed "correct" psy-choanalytic doctrine and practice, in some persons amounting to a smug certainty about issues which made me uneasy. We never discussed this area in our careful, formal, guarded "tolerance" for each other. Rigidity in form and practice, rejection of anyone else's beliefs should be anathema to therapists, as should resist-ance to what inhibits personal growth, freedom, doubts and ques-tioning.

Psychoanalysis can and must attempt to delineate the role, mechanism, theoretical tools and assumptions through which an idea of God may be approached, and states of psychical reality that are appropriate to or equivalent to the apprehension of what is known as the truth of God, or true self, or true being or "real presence".

Does human(un)kind need God or does God need man or each the other or neither either?

I am undecided. Most people need belief, God, religion and the relief belief brings from having to tolerate uncertainty, ignorance or the uncomfortable state of social dissonance and not belonging. Social life pressurizes towards conformity, including to a reli-gious belief system.

The theory of cognitive dissonance allows for each of the world's religions to be used as the disconfirming other while affirming its own beliefs. A particular religious affirmation (in which I include atheism, communism, even communalism) en-hances pressing individual and group human needs to belong, to conform, to obey whatever may be local beliefs and leading au-thoritative proponents. Affirming the local religion prevents the

pains of dissonance, alienation, non-conformity. Religious affiliation assures social continuity. Like psychoanalysis, religious ideas
give information about what is most important and interesting,
and grant life meaning. The majority of healthy, sane, thoughtful,
intelligent and mature human beings are not atheists and have
experiences that psychoanalysis is bound to examine.

Must "religious experience" necessarily evoke the explanatory hypothesis of the "Spirit of God"?

Many people experience the "urge" towards religious experience
and subject themselves to rigorous psycho–physical–spiritual exercises that Yogis and those who meditate practise. Expecting
nothing, because I needed quiet and undemanding time with myself in beautiful natural surroundings, after sitting several hours
daily for a week in full lotus position, breathing, trying to empty
my mind, disregard thoughts, and concentrate on trying solve the
"meaningless" and intellectually, cognitively insoluble (*Mu*) Koan
of the Rinzai Zen *zatsen* tradition at a retreat under the supervision of a "fully enlightened" Master of the Kyoto school, I was
surprised and privileged to experience what I can only describe in
words like "the opening of the gateless gate" or a pure, ineffable
experience of directly accessing my "pleasure centre". This master
told me that the experience was like a baby saying "mama" for
the first time: "Wait until you experience the Void!", he said. But I
decided that my quest for my "true nature" lay in other direc-
tions—especially after later experiences of meditation where instead I encountered what I regard as "the green meanies" aspect
of my potential experiential range. A Mahayana Buddhist friend
deemed my awesome experience "a sign of enlightenment", but
what did "the green meanies" betoken? I ascribe neither enlightenment, nor mystical, nor religious overtones to a seductive,
memorable experience that I would like to recapture at will but,
regrettably, cannot. One should not fear the awesome well-being
of such moments. I concur with Joseph Campbell's (1989) "follow
your ecstasy" advocacy. But, had I pursued the hint of my own
actualizable capacity for transcendent feeling states, I would not
be writing this.

Jung (1958) suggested that the function of religions is to protect us from an experience of God (!?). Spiritual excitement can
accompany sexual experience. Not only practitioners of Tantra
sometimes reach what others have described as "religious experience", whether or not such transcendent "peak" experience, peace
of mind, the world appearing new, is ascribed to an encounter
with the divine truth or sense of "soul". Deeply regressive experiences, close to religious experience, or an encounter with one's
"soul", "real self" or "truth" can occur during sexual intercourse
with cross-identificatory self-surrender. Certain Tantric practices
inextricably and explicitly interlink religious and sexual experience. When an Ituri forest pygmy dances ecstatically alone in a
glade, he probably is having a religious experience, but I doubt it
is sublimated sexuality. However, the religious experiences described by many ascetes do derive from an element of sublimated
sexuality.

Unreasoned enthusiasm in solemn emotion, self-surrender,
and awe characterize religious experience, which is different from
but related to mystical experience.

One may speculate psychoanalytically about *the basis for "religious" or "mystical" experience*. Pontalis (1981, p. 60) postulates
"the body's reflexivity"; reactivation of pristine memories taking
place with a concomitant "fantasy of circularity" with an externally perceived presence ("God"). This results in a psychosomatic
feeling of being in touch with profound and incommunicable
"true self" ("female element") continuity-of-being experience, in
Winnicott's terminology. Possibly memories are accessed from the
stage of primary non-differentiation, as by certain drug usage.

Speculative psychoanalytic "explanations" may be a basis for
our understanding "religious experience", but they cannot answer
questions about the existence or absence of God.

Does God exist?

The question is not an issue for psychoanalysis, which can only
comment about man—including everything man experiences,
does and thinks, and how and why we do or do not make use of
the rich complexities of our worlds. This may include/exclude

God and "spiritual" strivings and experiences. God may or may not exist whether or not man does or does not so believe, whether or not invented by man, whether or not as a necessity, and whether or not true religious belief begins with doubt. The concept "God" is itself but a metaphor of the unknowing mind, connotative not only beyond itself but beyond thought—not satisfactorily definable. All that can be said of it has to be in the way of an "as-if" observation, philosophically and theologically. Inexpressible, problematic, the concept of God remains plausible, useful and satisfying—probably necessary for us humans at this stage of our development. Yet it is not a totally necessary concept.

Winnicott (n.d.) hinted that perhaps from being God (as in dreams and play worlds) eventually human beings arrive at the humility proper to individuality. Can we equate "being God" with that childhood stage of hubris? Once we have reached the developmental stage when we can entertain the possibility of this far from primitive notion, how do we give up experiencing ourselves as being omnipotent/God? The question is based on an unverifiable assumption that may be wrong, namely that we (or babies) can experience ourselves as omnipotent/God when we are talking about a notion beyond our comprehension—the absurdity can be allowed for here . . .

The proposition that God exists may be true but by definition is one that surpasses human understanding. The kind of God the current scientific story gives us remains one in whom we can choose to believe or to disbelieve or, like myself, to be unconvinced in either direction and/or convinced in both.

Belief

Both belief and atheism can be repressed. Psychoanalysis sometimes (not necessarily) leads to renunciation of faith with clear understanding. Better understanding can also lead to better understanding of belief or of the way that basic human needs are met in certain religious rituals. Of course, faith can be renounced or belief justified without psychoanalysis.

I relate in both/and terms to the notion of God—as believer and disbeliever at the same time as neither!

How do we access or awaken higher levels of spirituality?

Such access or awakening comes from many different activities—from prayer, meditation in stillness and in movement, unexpectedly, from aesthetic experiences, visual or auditory, to asceticism and sexuality, even during psychoanalysis. Had space permitted, I would have presented illustrative clinical material from the analysis of a patient who felt that he had "recovered his very soul" during a particular session, although in this agnostic case no links to God were made.

On occasion I have practised ancient Eastern traditional exercises and experienced a (non-verbal) something that has led to a sense of deepest momentary vitality and peace. I would not quibble with those for whom such feelings have spiritual and cosmic connotations, but not religious ones. But I hesitate to claim the same for a humble non-adept like myself.

The meaning of Yehovah-God

In the Judaic tradition, God was named *Yehovah, Yud Heh Vav Heh* (meaning "to be, to be present, to take place, to turn out, to happen, to come forth", related to the root of the word for "experience"), in Hebrew shortened to *yud yud*, which stands for *Was–Is–and Will Be*. Generally this meaning is accepted as *eheyeh asher ehyeh*—translated either in present or future tense as *"I am present as I will be present"* or *"I am present as I am present"*—*"I am who am"* (Küng, 1981). Buber (1967) translated *Yehovah* as *"I will be present as I will be present"*. Towards the end of Jewish services, a hymn is addressed to *Adon Olam*, Lord of the Universe. The words say explicitly: He Was and Is and Will Be, before and after all created.

Winnicott's late formulations and Yehovah

With Winnicott's late formulations, psychoanalysis delves into the earliest areas of human development and draws attention to areas that directly connect to theological issues.

I was excited when I appreciated the significance of three profound ideas that Winnicott (1971b) put forward towards the end
of his life: (1) the inner subjective sense of an ongoing continuity-
of-being ("the lifeline"); (2) the way he described what he termed
"the female element" present in all men and in all women; and (3)
his earlier (1958) apperception of what he termed "true self—
whatever that is . . ." (my italics)—once discussed with me as his
"relief at discovering after eighteen years of analysis" that there
was a vital aspect of himself which "would remain forever incom-
municado and incommunicable".

These psychoanalytically derived Winnicottian concepts have
interesting parallels and relevance to diverse cultural mythologies
(in many cultures the ideas mean something similar, if not identical—e.g. Bantu, Delphic, Islamic, Confucian, Taoist, Buddhist,
Hindu). They are also directly related to the refined abstract
monotheistic Judaism's *Yehovah (Hayah, Hoveh-V'yehiyeh*—"Was–
Is–and Will Be"). *Yehovah* is alleged to have revealed him/herself
as "I AM" ("unit status"—an extremely important stage in
Winnicott's understanding of human development). No individual can say "I AM" in Hebrew—the present tense of the word
"to be" [*Liheyot*] is used solely in terms of God's existence.

In his terminological indecision, Winnicott hinted at his un-
formulated comprehension of the vast notion that his discoveries
touched on—namely, the complex issue of the inscrutable essence
of God. I read no assertion about the existence of a transcendental
God into Winnicott.

Mysticism

Pontalis (1981) noted that with Winnicott the word *being* enters
the world of psychoanalysis and that it is all too easy to avoid the
problem of its appearance by simply calling it pejoratively "mysticism". Pontalis "heard analysts claim that Winnicott was too
concerned with *being*, with the primordial position of 'I am', to
still be a psychoanalyst". This kind of dismissive certainty of attitude misguidedly rationalizes away a large issue. Psychoanalysts
cannot dismiss colleagues who note and discuss phenomena that

their analysands will certainly raise and experience and may not
be as well or even satisfactorily explained by whatever psychoanalytic theories they themselves hold.

Crucial mystical experiences have been described by too many
individuals for psychoanalysts to hold a dismissive attitude, as if
Freud's infantile regression to "oceanic feeling" hypothesis has
made it possible to regard all mystics as fundamentally infantile
and their thoughts accordingly of little significance or incomprehensible. It is clear that Winnicott himself was not of a mystical
bent from his tart *en passant* comment about Laing's (1967) *Bird of
Paradise*, together with his regret that Jung should have ended his
usefully productive life "in the futile pursuit of the centre of himself" (Winnicott, 1989).

The topic of mysticism is undoubtedly fascinating, but I prefer
to consider the manifold function that God serves, individually
and particularly, and generally, theoretically.

Making use of the idea of God

I hear Masud Khan's "God bless you!" as we part, my "Since
when do you believe in God?", and his swift response "But it's
such a convenient notion, don't you agree—*it leaves so much responsibility outside of one's own omnipotence!*" . . . Most certainly!

Winnicott (n.d.) wrote notes about a thoughtful child called
Tom who had lost his transitional object, "The Niffle", under
traumatizing circumstances. Tom wanted to know "What's God?"
His father tried to answer initially by illustrating with *true* things,
such as "Gravity is a *fact*. These things are God (etc. etc.)" reaching "a place where the answer was: 'We don't either of us know.
How did it all start? Well that's where God comes in'." Tom: "So *not
knowing*, that's God." To his mother, he said: "People don't know
why there's gravity so they say God made it. That's stupid. They
should say: *I don't know*."

Winnicott and Tom's mother listed different uses of God
"starting with idealisation . . . and ending . . . with the facts of
physics".

Winnicott (1989) stressed *the inherent paradox* in any transitional object "in that although the object was there to be found it was created by the baby". He linked this to

> the interminable discussion around the question: is there a God? If God is a projection, even so is there a God who created me in such a way that I have the material in me for such a projection? Aetiologically ... the paradox must be accepted, not resolved. The important thing for me must be, *have I got it in me to have the idea of God?—if not, then the idea of God is of no value to me (except superstitiously).* [p. 205, emphasis added]

Perhaps this is the most significant statement of Winnicott's concerning God. [*Mister God, This is Anna* (Fynn, 1974) provides a charming illustration; Beth, in Lars Von Trier's 1996 film *Breaking the Waves*, provides a self-destructive one.]

I will not dwell on the obvious ways in which the Almighty Protector and Judge, God, is paternalized or maternalized and personified via projections and imaginary projective identifications. "The term God is very much like the unstructured inkblot used in the Rorschach Test" (Rubenstein, 1992). All biblical Gods-(selves) are "gifts of the self" (Kristeva, 1987). We are not dependent on a wholly external God but are also inspired by our own Spirit-full nature.

Meissner (1984) expounded on *God as a transitional object*. As in this chapter, every subjective notion of God and religious belief is concerned with the subjective use of ideas as objects in the realm of transitional phenomena (Winnicott, 1958, 1971b, 1989) or as externalizations of the inner object world.

The clash between the supernatural and natural perspectives of the believer's faith is perhaps the most significant and least resolvable point of divergence between religion and psychoanalysis.

The supreme deity is endowed with *superego/ideal ego functions* by individuals and communities. Mankind needs ideals, needs to idealize, and needs gods, idols to idolize when not at ease with self-identity at an individual or social level. God is perceived as a symbol of the *ethical ideal*.

Use of the notion of God in relation to human destructiveness

I would like to stress the usefulness of the general perception of God as indestructible using Winnicott's distinction between object-relating and use of an object (Winnicott, 1971b, 1989). Even theologians who argue the Death of God theology acknowledge that this says nothing about the presumption that God exists. While not all humans form stable relationships to God or each other, the concept of an ongoing, indestructible Supreme Creative Spirit (God) is invaluable in maintaining a sense of difference between that which is beyond human intervention, comprehension, scientific exploration, explanation of nature and intervention in natural processes. This distinction is not less important than the maintenance of that between internal and external worlds, and belief in external reality. Belief that there really may be something that will survive human (omnipotent and fantasized) capacities for destructiveness is of some solace. Omnipotence becomes externalized and handed over to the notion of God as Supreme Being and Creator. The true-self part of original ongoing continuity-of-being is indestructible (Winnicott, 1971b, 1989), allowing for location of Yehovah-God also as inner and subjectively utilizable.

What remains experienced as internal, incommunicable, indescribable, inviolable, the core existential sense of being ("female element" or true self) is the soul of religious discourse, a profoundly significant reality. Whether located externally, analogous to what is known as Yehovah-God, or internally as that part of divine nature known as soul, it is beyond any individual or collective human "omnipotent" capacity to destroy in fantasy or actuality.

Surely the survival value of God beyond any of mankind's destructive capacity (which is vastly heedless, relatively puny, but nonetheless huge, certainly enough to destroy all life on this planet) plays an enormous role when we think of the value and function of God in our lives. Likewise nature/God's unimaginable destructive (and creative) power also brings us to a proper sense of our own humility.

Winnicott's (1989) comment about a remarkable dream that led him to understand that the way the world becomes experienced as external and real, distinguished from dream, and the inner world relieved of childish residues of omnipotence to develop a more or less successful capacity for perceiving, evaluating, and using external reality, including the notion of God, could be construed as a statement about a Godless creation of the human world.

Being alive in the presence of God. A believer who "walks with God" is never alone. A true believer with a firmly internalized and constant object-God, also experienced as God the (external) omnipresence, should never require an analyst in order to experience himself or herself as comfortably alone.

Making use of Almighty Yehovah-God for solace, healing, and restoration of the personal sense of continuity-of-being. The simplest definition of trauma can be stated in terms of anything that breaches the ego's defensive shield from outside and disrupts the sense of ongoing continuity-of-being whether intrasubjective, psychic, spiritual or physical, or extended to suprapersonal social and cultural realms, when support persons or the environment necessary for maintenance are disrupted so that individual physical or intrapsychic defensive, coping or resilience abilities are inadequate. In these conditions, trauma can be conceived of simply as any rupture(s) of the personal sense of inner-ongoing-being. Healing means, by bridging back to the pre-traumatized memory traces or condition, a restoration of the sense of continuity-of-being.

As generally envisaged, "God" as a continuity principle is beyond any such disruption. As such, God is important. Turning to God or the all-comforting arms of the Almighty for solace in times of trauma, loss, grief and pain is a natural and sometimes effective move towards healing, whether individual or in collective ritual.

A traumatized person can find solace, heal, when the "lifeline" sense of continuity-of-being is restored. The experience can be externally located as a projection when understood as an encounter with Almighty God.

To dwell with or in God is another function that God may play for humans "who cannot bear very much reality". Mending is sometimes ascribed to finding God when meaning is attributed to the experience.

Early types of mental functioning in relation to religious phenomena

The infant's experience of mother and identification with the mothering process occurs so early in development that it antecedes the availability of sufficient capacity for illusion necessary for the subjective self to play with the objective world in the "potential space" of transitional phenomena. A subject has to have achieved "a unitary self" to be able to use an objective object subjectively. Winnicott's notion of "female self" is in line with what Eastern teachers tell:

> The divine lives within you. Our Western religions tend to put the divine outside of the earthly world and in God, in heaven. But the whole sense of the Oriental is that the kingdom of heaven is within you. Who's in heaven? God is. Where's God? God's within you. And what is God? God is a personification of that world-creative energy and mystery which is beyond thinking and beyond naming. *That divinity which you seek outside, and which you first become aware of because you recognize it outside, is actually your inmost being.* [Campbell, 1989]

Personally I would feel impoverished without a capacity to experience such reverence.

In *The Future of an Illusion* (1927c), Freud raised the question, "If the truth of religious doctrines is dependent on inner experience which bears witness to that truth, what is one to do about the many people who do not have this rare experience?" Winnicott's contributions enable us to understand why such inner experiences are rare.

During the earliest stages of development, dependency on environmental provision and the effects of its quality is self-evident. Lack of "good-enough" care leads to personality fragmentation. *The answer to Freud's question may be because when such a dissociation or split exists, for the individual concerned the "female element" is not experienceable!* Accordingly, this whole area of conceptualization may be beyond the grasp of those, including eminent and useful psychoanalysts, who themselves are defending against "primitive agonies" by "flight to the split-off intellect"; a basic personality faulting, where existential and experiential "in-touchness" is missing or "female element" dissociation also exists such as is either explicitly discussed or hinted at by Winnicott (1960, 1989). This could explain some general conceptual–perceptual "closed-mindedness" and confusions prevalent in psychoanalysis.

The Shehinah

Psychoanalysts discover and re-discover basic human phenomena and describe them in like terms, difficult of definition as of apprehension. *Winnicott's concept of "the female element" present in all males and females bears obvious relevance to the complex ancient indwelling spirit, the* Shehinah, *in Judaism* (literally "dwelling", "resting", somewhat similar to the German word Freud used which was translated as "cathexis"). There have been many interpretations and usages of this concept, not dissimilar to the variations in the way Winnicott (1971b, 1989) discussed related phenomena in different places.

Winnicott's emphasis on the essential significance of "being as distinct from doing" is in line with metaphorical understanding of *Shehinah* defined as "absolute rest—the eternal ground for motion" (Cohen, 1929; following Maimonides, quoted by Küng, 1981). *Shehinah* is a female word. In *Kabbalah* (Jewish mysticism), *Shehinah* is described as "the daughter, princess, the feminine principle in the world of the divine *Sefirot* . . . while *Tiferet* and *Yesod* represent the masculine principle". "The main goal of the realm of the *Sefirot* (and of religious life as a whole) is to restore the true unity of God, the union of the masculine principle and the *Shehinah* which was originally constant and undisturbed."

Were I to believe in God, then I would have no difficulty with Zen Buddhism's insistence on introspective experiential knowledge as the only way to achieve spiritual development, or with Judaism's goals as understood by Maimonides—the practice of the 613 obligations [*mitzvot*] in the Bible (Leibowitz, 1989). I consider the *mitzvot* mnemonics for achieving higher consciousness, but rabbinically they are perceived as ways of helping observant practitioners to become open to God or receptive to the omnipresence of the *Shehinah*. Maimonides formulates the ultimate goal to which man should aspire as constant awareness of God and service of God through even mundane activities. Because God knowledge is the only knowledge worth having, all activities should be carried out with the aspiration of reaching knowledge-experience of God. This seems consistent with Zen practice as aspiration towards achieving the enlightenment of realizing *satori*—in atheistic Zen Buddhism, this is consistent with knowledge of "true self". Is this "true self" the same as Winnicott's "true self"? Or Winnicott's description of the "female element"?

In another group of Kabbalistic symbols, "the *Shehinah* is the battleground between the divine powers of good and evil; because of her femininity and closeness to the created world she is the first and main target of the satanic power" (Küng, 1981). This sounds close to Winnicott's statement about hatred against woman being primary because of hatred of having had to be born. I wonder if observance of certain *mitzvot* that are demanded only from men, certain prayer rituals, facilitate integration of male and female elements of the self in Winnicott's terminology?

Winnicott did not focus on the "religious" experiential *Yehovah* issue, although when he interpreted using the (even to him unsatisfactory) language of maleness and femaleness, he was close to this, as is evident in clinical material in "Playing: Creativity and the Search for the Self" (1971a). Winnicott reports how his patient speaks of her *"Returned Empty"* feeling state of not Being; her fear "Don't make me wish to BE!"; and explicitly of his "having taken away her God". Winnicott reports: "I referred here to *God as I AM, a useful concept when the individual cannot bear to BE"* (emphasis added).

How do we attribute location of God, self and experience?

Whether "God" is regarded as part of the human psyche or distinct from it, or the psyche itself as a manifestation of "God", neither depth psychology, nor theology, nor philosophy can answer, but the location of "god" can be examined in terms of the different realities encountered psychoanalytically.

"The self is not the centre; neither is it inaccessible, buried somewhere in the folds of being." Pontalis (1981) concludes that the self "is *found* in the *in-between* of outside and inside, the ego and non-ego, the child and his mother, the body and the word". This is precisely the description of and the ("potential space") area of transitional, including religious, phenomena.

Winnicott's finding/postulate of continuity-of-being can be considered in several ways, all relevant for the location of God:

a.   as a principle—if conceived continuity-of-being Was–Is–and Will Be Yehovah-God is locatable in the collective mind of mankind, our rich storehouse of external cultural [memes] collective consciousness, internally perhaps part of our collective unconscious archetypes or tribal memories;

b.   as an experiential sense, located innerly, termed part of the "true" self or an aspect thereof, the "female element", located in all of us;

c.   as located externally in all religious beliefs and doctrines;

d.   as both inner and outer in location;

e.   encountered in mythology in the area of transitional reality;

f.   conceived of as non-existent, as in the belief of atheism;

g.   considered as real, external, beyond human comprehension, as the notion termed "God" responsible for the creation/maintenance and re-creation of everything in universal and eternal terms.

Whether or not it is an integral part of the Yehovah-God notion as argued here, there is a basic need for a sense of continuity-of-being. Crapanzano (1992) pointed out that "much of what we in the West call psychological and locate in some . . . internal space ('head', 'mind', 'brain', 'consciousness') is understood in many cultures in manifestly non-psychological terms . . . located in other 'spaces'". Different cultures use other symbols, metaphors, and figures hung together differently: "To declare such articulations inadequate is an act of intolerable cultural arrogance. To reduce such articulations, as many psychoanalysts have, to some sort of projective mechanism of the established givens of psychological makeup is to perpetuate a closed system of thought and to ignore, if not the real possibility of human variation, then variations in human expression."

The "Death of God"?

After Auschwitz "we stand ... unaided by any purposeful power beyond our own resources. ... We live in the time of the death of God. This is more a statement about man and his culture than about God. The death (eclipse) of God is a cultural fact. ... Buber felt this ... 'the time which Nietzsche's madman said was too far off has come upon us'" (Rubenstein, 1992). This statement contains no denial of the existence of God: it is not an expression of atheism, although it rejects the biblical image of the God who elected Israel.

Rubenstein's post-Shoah psychoanalytic comprehension (1960, 1968, 1983, 1992; Rubenstein & Roth, 1986) of the functions of Jewish ritual is profound. He declares the Jewish God of yore dead in the face of *le vécu*, the Holocaust, but appreciates ritual practices as significant "cultural container" functions.

Rubenstein (1992) wrote: "Traditional Jewish theology maintains that God is the ultimate omnipotent actor in the historical drama. Traditionally every major catastrophe in Jewish history has been interpreted as God's punishment of a sinful Israel. ... To see any purpose in the death camps, the traditional believer is forced to regard the most demonic, antihuman explosion of all history as a meaningful expression of God's purposes." Thus *"the greatest single challenge to modern Judaism arises out of the question of God and the death camps"*. Anxiety is a direct consequence of our freedom. If there is no God then we alone are responsible for our actions. But *the assertion of radical theology that God is dead exceeds human knowledge. Such an assertion imparts knowledge of what the speaker believes. It imparts nothing about God.*

When I examined the extent of the need to establish continuities in human thought, I realized that it is of the order of a drive or instinct. *Yehovah is the over-reaching, all-embracing continuity.*

Is the death of God in contemporary thought in a sense "a wound of the order of being" (Buber, 1967) at a planetary level?

Is the notion of God necessary to "explain how it all started"?

What was there before time began? Science is no better able than theology and mythology to answer this ultimate question. Is this where scientific explanation breaks down and God takes over? The God notion or possibility is no more or less improbable than our own transient existence in this particular planet and galaxy in the incomprehensible vastnesses and infinite aeons of time. The presumption that God exists is as good as any other to explain how matter and anti-matter got there in the first place—perhaps a better one than "no explanation". Scientific explanations do not persuade me to believe one way or the other.

In conclusion

> "The greatest deception men suffer is from their own opinions."
>
> Leonardo da Vinci

I have ranged across a number of issues that concern psychoanalysis and mankind in relation to God and religion, with a particular emphasis on Judaism. I have presented some links that derive from Winnicott's ideas. Winnicott's "lifeline" sense of continuity-of-being is in essence identical to the traditional Jewish *Hayah-Hoveh-V'yehiyeh—Was–Is–Will Be Yehovah-God* (Issroff, 1983, 1993) which has dominated Western consciousness and history and is also well recognized and described in Eastern philosophical and religious traditions. Winnicott's (1971b) misleadingly named concept of "the female element" is a significant phenomenological, experiential and conceptual issue, an aspect of inner reality deriving from continuity-of-being. One way Winnicott used this notion is akin to the Jewish concept of *Shehinah*, the female aspect of Yehovah-God; it is akin also to the soul, with close affinity to Yehovah's inner "divine spark" manifestation.

Whether or not God exists is a matter of belief which neither psychoanalysis nor contemporary science can answer. "If God is a projection, even so is there a God who created me in such a way that I have the material in me for such a projection?" (Winnicott, 1989). Whether or not someone has the capacity to make use of the notion of God, and how, are the significant issues.

Acknowledgement: My thanks to Mrs. Ruth Rigbi for her patient, careful attention to clarifying my syntax and presentation.

CHAPTER EIGHT

A former Jesuit and an agnostic Jew talk about religion over a cup of coffee

Moisés Lemlij & Eduardo Montagne

Two psychoanalysts, Moisés Lemlij and Eduardo Montagne, met for coffee to talk about their experiences of and attitudes to religion, and to compare them. Each of them had prepared a small personal story which they used as the starting-point for the conversation.

Eduardo Montagne

I am a psychoanalyst and an Associate Member of the Peruvian Psychoanalytic Society. Religion is a subject that has been present in my life for as long as I can remember. The figure of my mother's brother, who was appointed Archbishop of Lima when I was still a child, had a deep and lasting effect on the religious atmosphere of my home. The Jesuit school that I later attended served only to reinforce this strong early family influence to the extent that, when I was 16 and had left school, I decided to respond to the "call of the Lord" and become a Jesuit priest.

At 16, I was unable to even intuit that this premature decision and the experiences of my childhood and adolescence could be directly related. I was "caught" by the religious discourse that attributes religious vocation to the will of God. It was only many years later that I was able to see that this decision, which marked my life so decisively from then on, looked to something external—the mysterious will of God—and not to something that I nurtured within me, such as desire or personal expectation. However, at the time, it would not have occurred to me to state that I wanted to be a priest because that was my wish. Nor did I suspect that this wish could be influenced by cultural, family, and historical conditioning; and less still by my apprehensions and fears, inhibitions, or personal convenience. It was only when I was well advanced in my personal analytic process that I was able to uncover a very complex range of personal motivations and outlines of the great ideals, prohibitions, fears, and inhibitions with which I had emerged from childhood.

I think that there is a fundamental advantage in attributing to God what is in fact the expression of a personal desire. It confers on one's personal plans a safe, permanent, and solid character, which is usually lacking in decisions taken on the strength of one's own wishes, as they are invariably subject to doubt, new developments, change, and uncertainty about whether they are right or wrong. If the decision is attributed to God, it assumes an almost superhuman strength and an unquestionable certainty which, in my case, was reinforced by the religious discourse of the time. "If God calls you"—my spiritual guides would say—"there is no possible doubt, and all that you can do is accept his call and follow him." Besides, the idea of having been worthy of God's notice, and favoured with a vocation that reminded me of the great calls of the Bible, satisfied my adolescent narcissism.

The sense of security that religion provides is tremendously important at certain times of life, such as adolescence. Many possibilities and alternatives are opened up, but accompanied by a large dose of uncertainty and insecurity. I chose a path that offered me such security and also enabled me to receive the admiration, applause, and recognition of my teachers, my family, and some of my friends. They saw in this choice a halo of greatness of soul and heroic generosity, and I became an object of admiration in a culturally religious milieu that put great value on this sort of gesture.

I began my education in the Company of Jesus at 17 and spent several long years in study, reflection, and meditation and with very little contact with the outside world. This isolation seemed quite normal to me then, but now I consider it contradictory. It is rather illogical to study philosophy (for example) while mentally and physically cloistered—as if it were possible to develop one's thought exclusively among those who share the same philosophical theses, viewing any other current of thought as belonging to the "opposition" or to "adversaries".

Hence my inner assurance was due, to a great extent, to the exclusion of the diverse and the different, characteristics not only of religion but of any militancy. I received my religious training in the 1960s and 1970s, a time marked by political and ideological militancy . . . by the Berlin Wall. Curiously, in that sense, I was not indifferent to the cultural climate of the time. I pursued a sort of religious militancy that required a commitment and deeply held truth, which gave me considerable personal security. For me, there were no different or complementary truths: there was only one truth, which I had the privilege to know and the responsibility to make known. Like all militancy, my religious commitment sealed me off from any questioning that arose from outside my confined world. So it was that throughout my youth I took refuge in something that could be likened to the *Titanic*, whose apparent invulnerability allowed me to sail in troubled waters with no sense of danger.

What was it, then, that led me to begin analysis and my first psychotherapy training after eleven years of priesthood and twenty-one years after I first entered the Jesuit seminary?

My explicit motive, the one that I presented to others, was a growing interest in being better able to understand the problems of which people spoke when they came to me for emotional and psychological help. I had always been very interested in counselling, in listening, and in having personal contact with adults, young people, couples, and families; but I also had the feeling that there were psychological and emotional aspects of life which I did not understand.

Nevertheless, in the course of the analytic process I had to admit—not without great effort—that I had looked for help simply because I needed it, because it was a clamour that arose within me and that I felt deeply. I found it difficult to express myself, with all letters in place, and to say: "I want to undergo serious and profound analysis because I am in need of it." This clarity in formulating my wishes was quite foreign to me by virtue of a mechanism that concealed my own inner truths or needs behind a robe and linked them to my work or to doing good for others or to further training. It was much easier for me to say: "I want to do my psychoanalytic training to help others and to understand the problems of others." Anyway, concealed or not, today I know that the desire to find other perspectives in my life was there for many years but had always been postponed.

My Jesuit studies took me from Lima to Madrid, to Mexico and to Rome. But it was in my psychoanalytic studies where, for the first time, I shared an academic and intellectual exercise with a heterogeneous group of men and women, of different ages and backgrounds, where the issue of religion was not explicit in the least, far less the reason for the meeting taking place. For me it was a confrontation with the diverse, with the new, with the supposition that I needed to account for my own reality. This reality, of being a Jesuit and of the clergy, was no longer something to be accepted as obvious but was instead the subject of curiosity and questions.

How did I experience my religious faith during psychoanalysis? I entered into my analysis with the image of a God who judged according to two categories, "good" and "bad", and who established what we must do or not do, always in connection with high ideals, guilt, and the threat of punishment—a superego God who, from that position, exercises his strength and power. The attentive and respectful listening, the analytical neutrality, the chance to express myself without restriction, to say whatever occurred to me in my free association, being neither judged nor criticized, was completely new to me.

Analysis led me to a different experience of God. A God who gradually lost the Superego image and became instead more internal, personal, and creative. A God who was nearer to the world of desires, of fantasies, of freedom; a God who imposed fewer constraints and who, on the contrary, gave much more opportunity to be, to think, to imagine, to create, and to love. A God who allowed both the autonomy to take personal decisions, and the responsibility to run risks and take the consequences. In sum, from the point of view of the believer, I stopped being a child in the presence of God the Father and became an adult whose father allows him the space necessary for his autonomy.

I believe that it was during my analysis that I came to understand the transcendence of God; I learned to relate to a divine image that was beyond my own life, my personal decisions, my mistakes, my guilt, or my successes. A divine image who allowed me to dwell in the home of humans without having him as an intrusive and time-consuming guest. All this involved a growing experience of freedom, autonomy, and personal realization which had opened the way for the appearance of my own plans and desires—not just those of that particular time, but also those that had in some way been latent for many years but had been repressed or put off by the presence of a God who, in my previous experience, had been overwhelming.

As might be supposed, this also involved the conflict, pain, and uncertainty that generally accompany any major transformation. The image of a transcendent God who lets people live, who is closer to the id than to the superego of the personality, came up against the kind of institutionalized relations with God, proper to the church in general, that I had previously established. The strong feeling of belonging to my religious order broke down when I confronted aspects of the institution which I could not reconcile with what I was discovering in myself. This obviously caused considerable pain as, through the years, I had made links of a deeply human nature—friendship, companionship, closeness, solidarity—with many of my Jesuit colleagues.

My first reaction was to deny the difference and conflict. I tried to sustain the belief that, in my case, it would be possible to be both a Jesuit and a psychoanalyst at the same time, that the difficulties that I encountered would be resolved after finishing my analysis, and that it would always be possible to form a synthesis. But this utopian synthesis never came into being, because what was personally convenient, healthy, and creative from the analytic perspective was reprehensible, suspect, or inconvenient from the church perspective, and vice versa. These were not two parallel lines but diverging lines and I could travel in only one direction. Yet to advance along one path would entail an internal split.

Inevitably, the moment came when I had to make a choice. I resolved to follow the direction that, for me, meant life, personal realization, humanity, and affective plenitude. The new image I had of God no longer meant that I had to sacrifice these objectives. On the contrary, the attempts to achieve them stimulated me to seek further. So I left the Jesuits and the army of the priesthood, applied for the licences and permits of day-to-day life, and began to live personally and autonomously. Some time later I married. Today I feel I am leading a full life, a life that is personally and professionally integrated. I am no longer putting off my personal realizations for some time in the future.

So what is left of my belief? Does analysis necessarily lead one to abandon religious experience? I would say that the Titanic in which I was so comfortably sailing sank. The institutional ecclesiastical world had been, for me, the greatest, safest, and most beautiful ship in the world, which no one—not even God Himself—could sink. But that personal Titanic hit the iceberg of a non-ecclesiastical world, with the generically different, the diverse—and it sank. Everything that I had until then related to faith within the framework of the institutional church sank. I had been too far gone in ecstatic contemplation of the Titanic's safety, beauty, and self-possession to realize that it could hit the iceberg entailed by the confrontation with the challenging aspects of otherness.

Did my faith also go down with my personal Titanic? Was the faith that I professed, and which is in some way part of my identity, also wrecked with my ecclesiastical Titanic? And if the answer is *No*, what is this faith that I now experience, no longer from the imposing majesty of the Titanic but from the humble instability of my fragile personal boat?

When friends ask me if I am still a believer, I say that I am—quickly adding—"in my own way". After the intense personal crisis that was inevitable and also—I maintain—very healthy, after the certainties dissolved and I found other ways of self-affirmation and of affirming my own identity as a believer, with less pretension, without the backing of an institution, without "militancy" or the appearance of solidity, today I believe from the most genuine and personal roots of my being. I believe that belief is not incompatible with analysis. I also believe that analysis can lead to an openness to transcendence, precisely because it puts one in contact with that which is beyond appearances, beyond what is manifest, what is conscious—in general, beyond everything. The unconscious is radically different and, if anything, seems to be nearer to the "absolute other"—the term that theology uses to describe God.

Moisés Lemlij

I am a psychoanalyst belonging to both the Peruvian Psychoanalytic Society and the British Psycho-Analytical Society. My parents fled Eastern Europe and came to Peru in the mid-1930s. They were very different from Lima's small Jewish community in one important way—they were left-wing. My father remained so to the end of his days. My mother, who is now 85, is still a socialist.

For some it might seem paradoxical that my parents were also traditionalists. But not to them, because they understood that being Jewish defined their national and cultural identity rather than being a religion, which they considered "the opium of the people" and a part of the particular political system against which they fought. They thought that non-believers were intellectually superior, and they showed a marked antagonism towards everything religious. In the atmosphere in which I grew up, political dogmas replaced those of religion.

Although I was afraid of making my father extremely irritated, I would slip off on Jewish Holy Days to visit an old uncle who would give me pocket-money if I went to the synagogue. Even then, it was obvious to me that the ceremonies that I attended with such curiosity were rituals not far removed from those held by adherents to political doctrines. At university, I gradually grew away from my family's political dogmas. I remember my father saying—half-serious and half-joking—"I cannot understand how I managed to have such a reactionary son". When I started studying medicine and then psychoanalysis, I felt fully identified with Freud's conception of both religion and ideologies in general which he mainly developed in *The Future of an Illusion* (1927c) and *Civilization and its Discontents* (1930a).

During my analysis, I suffered a profound personal crisis. Whilst this experience was intense, I could not say that it had religious connotations. The issue of transcendence was theoretical; I have never thought of myself as being particularly sensitive and it did not touch me personally. Whenever—in my youth or as an adult—I have suffered the pain of losing relatives or friends, it was an experience of loss and the terrible pain of loss. But it was not until I had another kind of experience with death, which I lived through as an analyst with patients who faced its imminent approach, that I felt deeply moved. I felt that the advance knowledge of the death of the person with whom I spoke put me in communication with "something". I cannot say that I am now a believer, but I do think and feel differently following these experiences.

The first of these events concerned a 22-year-old patient who had been saved from a massive overdose of paracetamol which he had taken to end his life. He had not been able to bear the change from being an excellent pupil at secondary school to a repeated failure at a well-known university and being just another student. He preferred facing death to the pain and humiliation involved if his parents found out about his poor performance. I recommended that he be admitted to hospital since it was highly probable that he would attempt suicide again in view of the severe depression he was suffering. But both the patient and his parents insisted on his being discharged, and they willingly signed a form indicating that he had left hospital against the advice of his doctor. One month later, I was called to identify a body that had been washed up by the river. It was my patient.

There was something that I could have done for this young man that might have changed the course of things: I could have applied to a judge for an order for compulsory admission to hospital, a trying procedure. Even now, I do not know whether I did not do it out of lack of energy, mistaken judgement, or because such is life. But the face of the boy, both when he was alive and that of his dead body, come to my mind more often than I would like.

The second case was a homosexual patient with whom I had occasional follow-up interviews once his analysis was over. One day he came with the positive result of his HIV test, and he said to me—"Look, all of us are going to die, including you and me. This only means that it is going to happen to me a bit sooner." Apart from the sorrow I felt, I was astounded by his reaction: was this a massive denial, or did he feel a kind of relief because, with the announcement of his death, he began to settle a hidden debt with one of his ghosts from the past?

My third experience of this kind was with a long-standing patient who rang me from a clinic where he had recently undergone an operation for cancer, two years after he had finished analysis. He wanted me to help him find the strength to fight for his life. During our interviews, I was deeply moved when he began to recognize the inescapable nature of his death, and began to accept it and to work with me to be at peace with himself. One day he told me of a dream in which he saw me in an auditorium presenting a talk on the sessions that we had before his death. His tale gave me the impression that he was looking for a way to prolong his life, to see what would happen when he was no longer there. Taking his leave at the end of that session, which was to be the last, he said: "I am grateful to you for all you have taught me, it's a pity I have no time to use it." He died two weeks later.

For some reason, the experience of accompanying these men to their deaths, and the rapport I established with them, has meant that they continue to be present—and therefore alive—in my mind and that I have a very strange communication with them. It isn't that I believe in the Here-After. The link that I established with them, as their analyst, was one of fusion. As the participating-I and not merely the observer, I shared with them the feelings that accompanied their remembrances about important moments in their lives, their anticipated sense of missing their loved ones whom they will no longer see; their disappointment at not having done a number of things and their anger at no longer being able to do them, their infinite sadness; the way they valued and enjoyed their simple daily moments, which they now found beautiful and full of meaning; their fears, their cynicism, their impotence, their inner heartbreak, their suppositions about what would happen after their death, their serenity and resignation— well, all the ideas and feelings that the nearness of death provoked in them. I had—and still have—the chance to experience a very special sensation of being in contact with the transcendent which I would describe in a form very similar to the religious experience of the feeling of being one with the whole, the roots of which Freud traces back to the oceanic sentiment of the fusion of the baby with its mother, proper to primary narcissism.

A cup of coffee

Moisés: The first thing that comes to my mind after this exchange of personal experiences is that it is possible to establish a difference between the link with the transcendent (not necessarily with a god) and the rituals with which each religion attempts to symbolize it. In some cases, the emphasis on the ritual aspect is such that the link with the transcendent seems to be lost. You lived religious experience from the cradle but I would say that, with the passage of time and after profound personal change, you left the ritual side behind, with all the paraphernalia that surrounded your faith, and you kept what is for you essential and transcendent. This reminds me of Ezra Pound when he asked his students to write a poem and then asked them to cut it down to just the final sense—the essence.

Now, I never had any religious education. Perhaps my experience with politics could be considered the equivalent of ritual and idealization but, for me, this never meant contact with the transcendent. Whereas the "non-personal" pain of my experiences as an analyst, of patients with a demand that could be expressed as "Interpret my fatal illness, heal me with your divine interpretation!", brought me face to face with an appalling sensation of powerlessness, and could be so described. For me, it was not enough simply to follow the technical recommendations and "accompany them" in this time of trouble. I would have liked to be able to say to them: "I will give you a couple of years of my life."

I know that many doctors experience this feeling. But I am convinced that the patient–analyst experience is different because the intensity of the link is so much greater, especially since it is registered on a symbolic level. The analyst can end up fusing with the patient to such an extent that—as in my case—I would say that he or she transcends what is pure projection, what we call projective identification or fusion of representations.

It may have been this experience that led me to an "incipient" religious feeling. I do not affirm this, or wish it to develop, but I do know that it has put me in contact with something new, something I had not met before, which transcends the limits of my self, of my own existence, and which is nevertheless deep inside me. Not even love—not only in terms of a partner, but also love of my children and parents—has brought me close to the unlikely window that has since enabled me to participate in this other level of experience.

Eduardo: What you are saying has given me an interesting idea regarding our different approaches to religious belief. I think what you say is true. In my case, I had to set aside many things to be able to discover what I feel is "authentic"—or, at least, to try to do so. You did not need to give up anything because you had no initial family experience of this. Instead, you brought "something" to the experiences which you have described about the deaths of some of your patients that made them special and significant.

This reminds me of the image of the painting and sculpture which Freud used to describe analytic therapy. With reference to religious experience, what is it that leads more directly to an encounter with the authentic? Taking down the "artificial" scaffolding that could not be considered "authentic", or, as in your own case, painting onto a blank canvas the characteristics of one's own experience, could, in this sense, certainly correspond to what one has felt and perceived, to something authentically one's own.

Moisés: I think that is a good metaphor. I'll go further: I have always had to treat my patients who are in religious orders with great care. I have treated a Roman Catholic priest and a Rabbi who both reaffirmed their faith throughout their respective analyses. I am also reminded of a nun who fell into a depression when the habit which those of her Order wore was changed. She felt vulnerable and threatened; she had an institutional conflict. After analysis, she went back to her work as a missionary, which she did magnificently. I never doubted her faith or vocation. I simply applied the techniques, letting her find her own way.

Nevertheless, patients who know themselves to be near death provoke something that may mean a profound change in the self or essence of the analyst. This is not only because the structural and representational is at stake, but also the very essence of the patient's being. The overwhelming thing is that we are not dealing with a metaphor—we are talking about dying.

I could say that, in my case, bits of myself, black holes, began to be filled with their absence, an absence that I already felt even before they had died. I did not cry but I did feel a profound pain, as if I were losing something very close to me. It is a different pain, not like that produced by the death of a friend or a loved one or any other pain. No doubt you and I have both suffered during terrible times of crisis. But the space left in my mind as a result of the heartbreak caused by these patients has been populated by their presence which I now feel as a part of myself. They go on living in my mind, and it is this feeling that moves me and I identify it as my link with the transcendent.

Eduardo: Would you say then that, in someone like yourself, who has no past or present religious representation, there is still a sort of nucleus from which a kind of personal, unique, and untransferable—and possibly indescribable—transcendent experience can spring? I am asking this because you said that in you personal analysis the subject of transcendence, belief, or religion never arose.

Moisés: Never, never . . .

Eduardo: That "never", what does it mean exactly? It didn't arise because it didn't exist, or because it was a repressed part of you that had simply not found a time to come out? I have read an article by a German author who states that Freud simply re-

pressed his faith and that this opened up paths from the unconscious, in roundabout ways and against his explicit will, into his
life and his doctrine. In other words, there might be a repressed
or encapsulated faith. What do you think of that?

Moisés: If I had not treated those patients, I would have said that it
was either something repressed or non-existent. Now I believe
that there is something that must be touched for it to appear. In
my case, it had to be the sum of all my experience with each of
the three patients I have described. With the first, I had a sensation that stayed with me. But I needed the experiences with the
other two patients for this to take some form. I even had to write
about it, just something short, to get it clear in my mind.

But for me the question still remains whether this is something that people have and repress, or whether it is something
that one only experiences as a result of a constellation of events,
i.e. something that is beyond oneself. I personally also wonder
whether having experienced this particular kind of pain with
my patients, and having had this experience which I have
linked to the transcendent, has enriched me. I have not had a
mystical experience that has inspired me to write poetry like St.
Theresa or the Gospel like St. John, although who would not
wish to write as well as they? But, I repeat, my experience is not
a mystical one, it is an experience of transcendence.

Clearly, my experience cannot compare with yours, which is
unique. There must be many analysts, particularly in Latin
America and in some European countries, who would find my
experience familiar: no religious past, some sort of political activity. Perhaps not in the United States. Whereas your experience is something I am sure is fascinating to everyone.

Eduardo: It's fascinating as fireworks are fascinating, but I find
your experience much more thought-provoking from the point
of view of formulating a postulate of transcendence and trying
to describe it as aseptically as possible. My case involved taking
down a very complex scaffolding of religious representations,
giving up ritual and the use of words learned or even imposed.
In your case, we can see an attempt to put into your own words,
with the modesty and charm we can expect, something that is
and remains genuinely yours.

I think that, as an experience, this postulates a certain open-ness to the transcendent—that which is new, different, call it what you will—without having to bring it into line with the beliefs of others or with a theology or to accompany it with what you call religious paraphernalia. I am not sure that many analysts will want to think about these experiences which bor-der on the religious. It is much easier to say "I am not a be-liever", "I am an atheist", or "I am an agnostic" than to say "I am not religious, but there is something that makes me think about religion" and try to put into words what you feel, how-ever provisionally.

My own personal experience makes me search for the needle in the haystack—that is, the authentic in the midst of the myriad mental representations that people my mind, some of which are no longer valid. But I do believe that there is a needle in the haystack, and I have not yet stopped searching for it.

Conclusions

It does not seem easy to put an end to this conversation. Maybe because we would like to continue drinking coffee . . . to continue exchanging our experiences on the theme. Something that we both believe is that, after going through a long analysis, what bound us in the theme is not the convergences or the divergences that separate us. Rather, it is the possibility to bring closer such different experiences, experiences that are not usually disclosed in conversations between colleagues. We believe that the eager-ness for searching and the honesty to question oneself, which is not always easy, are aspects that have made our coffee so aro-matic and our conversation so enriching.

CHAPTER NINE

The Spirit of God

Colin Murray Parkes

"The profoundest of all infidelities is the fear that the truth
will be bad."

Herbert Spencer

In my childhood, my view of God was a reflection of my view of
my family. A source of security and all good things. I was
fond of God; God as Santa Claus, God as Father, God as Love.
God knows, I met him everywhere and he was reassuring and
safe. God's in his heaven, all's well with the world.

In my youth, I began to doubt this simplistic view. I put off
childish things, left home, and tried to stand on my own two feet.
"Independence" was the watchword, and I tried to become independent of God just as I tried to become independent of my
father. Like my father, God was fallible—in fact, he had a lot to
answer for. I challenged his goodness (why did he allow bad
things to happen?), his partiality (why should he have chosen one
race in preference to another?), his vanity (why should he need to
be worshipped?), his consistency (why should he establish Laws

of Nature in order to break them by performing miracles?), his origins (did man make God in his own image?), his authorship of the Bible (did he really order bears to tear forty-two little children because they insulted one of his prophets—Kings II:2:24?), his sex (why should God not be female or bisexual?), and, in the end, his existence.

As a child I had been taught that FAITH (i.e. believing what I was told) was a virtue for which I would be rewarded in heaven; as a young man and a scientist I learned that this kind of uncritical faith was a vice and that all faith should be based on logical appraisal of evidence. When I tried to apply this approach to the evidence for most of the dogmas of my religion, I found that house of cards collapsing. Confusing religion with belief in God, I declared myself an atheist.

Yet, even in my most angry and iconoclastic moods, I could not get away from doubt. I picked away at God; I read books on the historical roots of the Bible as if, by proving that sacred books were flawed, I could prove that God was equally unworthy. If my atheism had been a firm conviction—I would not have bothered.

I challenged my clergy friends to answer my complaints against God and found, to my surprise, that many of them had the same doubts. My friends did not try to prove to me that their religion was the only true faith; they refused to argue whether God should be called "God" or "Allah" or "Rah"; they suspected that all religions were, in some sense, true. So what *did* they believe? The answers that I got, and continue to get, have more to do with searching than with finding, *with seeking for a meaning in life and ending with something called God.*

Part of the problem lies in the act of naming. By naming something we attach a particular meaning to it. We give it individuality, we distinguish it from other objects or concepts having different names. We pin it down.

Yet *God cannot be pinned down*, and any attempt to limit God distorts God. All definitions of God limit God. The ancient Jews recognized this difficulty when they asserted that the name of God was too holy to be uttered. It would seem to follow that all discussion of God, including this book, belittles God.

I confess to having some sympathy with this argument and to have had some misgivings about contributing to the book for this very reason. However, the alternative is to forgo discussion of God, and this may have the same effect. It may be necessary to run the risk of misrepresenting God if we are to discuss the issues at all. All we can do about this is to make ourselves conscious of the danger.

A peculiar form of belittling, which can be useful if it points up the nature of the problem, is humour. Jokes about God have always been regarded with suspicion. Yet the "Monty Python" approach that brings out the silliness of much of our sanctimonious posturing may help to focus our attention on the things that matter.

Questions for which my knowledge of science provided no answers included questions about ultimate meaning. If we ask "What is the meaning of God?", a possible answer is *"Meaning is the meaning of God"*.

When John Freeman, in the television programme "Face to Face", asked Carl Jung "Do you believe in God?", Jung replied: *"I don't believe—I know."* In that simple statement he encapsulated the whole issue. If God is meaning, then if we know meaning we know God. Descartes's datum "I think, therefore I am" could thus be recast, *"I think, therefore God is"*. Our own direct evidence of meaning can only stem from our own thought, the function of our minds, and we know that this is meaningful.

Applying the "Monty Python Test" to this we come up with the question *"What is the meaning of meaning?"*, a subject to which philosophers have paid a great deal of attention (see, for instance, Ogden & Richards' 1972 tome on the subject). In the end, I suspect that we cannot do better than accept that *the meaning of life is the meaning that each one of us finds in it*—"The Life I am trying to grasp is the me that is trying to grasp it" (R. D. Laing, 1957). This is very variable, with some perceiving great order and richness while others see little but chaos. It leaves us with very little consensus of belief, certainly no more than a very shaky beginning to a search for a God that is individual to each person.

Among the universal concepts that give meaning to life are the Laws of Nature: regularity, predictability, and systems which we perceive and which can be classed as concepts of Order. Another set of concepts having to do with meaning consists of such concepts as Justice, Beauty, and Goodness. These are concepts of Worth or Value. Hence we have *two aspects of God: God as the orderer of all things and God as ultimate value.* I think that I experience God in both these aspects when I gaze at a beautiful landscape or watch my grandchildren at play.

While we may have considerable difficulty in agreeing about the precise meaning, in either order or value terms, of any particular experience or object, we would probably agree that our lack of consensus stems from the fact that each of us has a different experience of life and sees the world in a different way from the experience of others. Our perception of meaning is limited by our experience, and this can never be more than partial since we are incapable of perceiving, let alone understanding, more than a very small part of the universe.

This may explain why there are many aspects of life which, to us, seem to reflect chaos rather than order and negative values such as injustice, ugliness, and badness rather than worth. Do we need to postulate an Anti-God or Devil to account for these phenomena, or are they simply a reflection of our own ignorance or blindness? It seems to me that it is the second of these explanations that makes the most sense. Creating devils seems too much like shifting the blame.

It is as if in our lifetime each one of us is given a glimpse of a small part of the pattern of an immense carpet. We know that the carpet extends far beyond our range of vision and that each one of us sees a different part of it, although our views also overlap. We see this view of God most clearly by climbing mountains, gazing at the night sky, or peering through a microscope. On the basis of this experience, both individual and shared, it is reasonable to extrapolate that *there is a greater whole of which we are a part and that the parts that we cannot perceive must also have a pattern, a meaning.*

The danger with this kind of thinking is that it gives us a very remote, theoretical, and awesome view of God. *God is just too big for us.* It is difficult to imagine big God out there taking the slightest interest in little me. Yet if God is involved in all things, God is involved in me and in a sparrow and in a grain of sand. Perhaps it is for this reason that we need to bring God down to earth. In most faiths, this is done by locating God in a particular person or other object who then acts as a link with the big God out there. *Our household Gods may be less credible, but they are far more lovable than God in Majesty.*

Children do something similar when they play. Dangerous animals are reduced to teddy bears and plastic dinosaurs, dollies are taken to hospital and cured by nurses and doctors, battles are fought with alien spacecraft. The fact that these toys are not to be taken seriously does not mean that they are not valuable ways of beginning to relate to, and to gain control of, the real world. Children of other animal species develop their physical and mental skills by mock fights and hunts. Human children go far beyond this in the complexity and sophistication of the games they play.

But play does not end with childhood. At all ages we spend time playing with ideas and the symbols that embody them. In reverie and in dreams, and in interaction with the books and other media that we seek out, we try to come to grips with the real and imagined problems that we face. Sometimes this is done at a realistic problem-solving level, at others it takes on the qualities of playing with a problem in a way that appears remote from the real world but, even so, has important connections with it.

One phenomenon, the meaning of which we find particularly difficult to understand, is death. None of the great world religions is at all specific about what lies beyond this life; an act of faith is always necessary if we are to move confidently into the unknown. *Our ability to cope with the prospect of our own death is, perhaps, the acid test of faith.*

As a psychiatrist who has spent much of his life working with people who are faced with serious illness, death, and bereavement, I have become familiar with the difficulties inherent in facing up to this problem and the ways in which we do this by what Avery Weisman (1972) calls "double knowledge". When people have cancers or similarly life-threatening illness, they often oscillate between times when, for a while, they will speak frankly and openly about the likely fatal outcome of their illness and times when they assert that they are getting better and develop elaborate fantasies to explain their symptoms; these distort reality and come closer to play than to rationality. Doctors learn that, in order to help people to cope with the situation, they need to be tolerant of such behaviour, to deliver momentous information in "bite-sized chunks", and to allow people time to "play through" their fears.

These problems exist even when one is not in immediate danger of dying, for we are all mortal; hence, perhaps, the frequency with which death and threats of death appear in the media. Geoffrey Gorer (1965) dismisses this as the "pornography of death", but this judgemental attitude disallows the possibility that playing with death is a creative and potentially valuable activity, a way of living with dying. By fictionalizing death, we make it remote enough to be examined. Even so, we play death games most happily when we are fit and healthy and not under direct threat.

The idea of another world outside of this one to which we go when we die—a world where justice, peace, and understanding prevail and where we come closer to God—is one of these games and is an idea that most of us come close to believing. In the light of the carpet metaphor described above it, may not be so unlikely as it sounds. Yet I am uncomfortable with a heaven that sounds too much like a reflection of my wish to believe that the next chapter of existence will necessarily be better than the last.

Because the transition from life to death is a transition into an existence of which we know very little, it is hard to prepare for it. We know that life can be painful, and that the illnesses and accidents that precede death increase the risk that we will suffer. Consequently we dread the possibility that death too will be painful, almost as if any suffering that occurs at the moment of death will be protracted forever.

Reflection shows this fear to be unjustified. Pain and grief are mental activities peculiar to living organisms and useful to those organisms in helping them to avoid danger. As death approaches and cerebral activity becomes impaired, any pain that may have been present dwindles, and the integration of higher mental functions that cause both physical and mental pain is ended by death. Consequently, we should fear death less than a journey into an unknown part of this world which may, indeed, be hazardous and painful. Any fear that remains is a reflection of our own distrust and our wish to stay in control. This can be countered if we seek for, and find reasons for, trusting in the meaning of existence.

It seems to me that *only if we can find meaning and value in the known world can we trust that there will be meaning in the unknown.* To do that we may need to take a broad perspective. True, there are many times when individuals must suffer and there are times when one fears that such suffering will go on for ever. Even so, most creatures, most of the time, find the food, warmth, love, and companionship as well as the other necessities which make existence worthwhile.

In the environment in which mankind evolved and in which the blueprint of our psychology was established, threats to life, death, and bereavement occurred frequently, and we evolved an entire nervous system, the Autonomic System, to enable us to cope with them. Maybe we in the "developed countries", who now live in a world that is safer than it has ever been, have developed a distorted view of suffering and of death. We have been so successful in our efforts to abolish these things from our life plans that we see them as aberrations in God's plan; we no longer recognize them for what they are: necessary conditions for this chapter of our existence.

Of course, it is not only our own death that we fear, but also the deaths of those we love. Indeed, there are many who can accept the prospect of their own death with equanimity yet who are completely thrown by the loss of someone they love. For them, it is easier to die than to survive. Here, too, the *need to find ways of making real the intolerable reality we face may cause us to play games, not as an escape from grief but as a way of beginning to make sense of it and to cope with it.* Thus many bereaved people experience a strong sense of the presence of the dead person near at hand. They may not be seen, heard, or touched, but this does not prevent them from being located in particular places where the bereaved can find some comfort in being close to them. It is easy to dismiss such experience as wish-fulfilling fantasy and there may well be an element of this involved, but there is another sense in which this "game" can be seen as a way of facilitating the transition from an attachment to a bodily person outside of ourselves to a new relationship with the internal representation of the loved person whom we carry within us. There is a literal truth in the statement "He (or she) lives on in my memory". Unfortunately, our desperate need to get someone back "out there" can blind us to the fact that we never lost them "in here". Mementoes, visits to the grave, and the cultivation of this sense of presence help us to let go of the external reality and discover the internal.

In like manner, our inability to perceive or relate to the invisible and unthinkable nature of God may explain our efforts to reify God as a man, a father, a son, or a mother. We should, however, be aware that none of these images or symbols of God is more than a very partial glimpse of the whole. God has many faces. *One man's symbol is dismissed as an idol by another, yet each may have a symbolic "truth" which transcends reason.*

If the spirit or essence of God is to be found in the meanings that we find in life, it is inextricably bound up with issues of life and death. Science may not tell us much about what lies beyond this life, but it can tell us something if we are prepared to go back to first principles. The mystery of *what happens to my identity when I die* has puzzled human beings from time immemorial; less attention has been focused on the question of *what happens to my identity while I am alive.* I am a multi-cellular animal controlled by a central nervous system. Individual cells of my body are dying each day, and that includes cells in my central nervous system. While most of those body cells that die are replaced, this is not the case in the central nervous system of the adult human. Each day the ageing process is carrying out small lobotomy operations. My sense of identity is an illusion: *I am not the man I was.*

My mind resides in my brain and reflects its functioning. My memory, speed of thinking, and ability to process complex information is not what it used to be, and I would not stand a chance of winning a "shoot-em-up" computer game against my children. The fact that, despite this, I continue to learn and to accumulate experience gives me advantages over my children in other respects. I am, or should be, wiser and more experienced than them in many ways and, indeed, wiser and more experienced than the me that I was when I was their age.

If I live long enough, however, I shall find that the losses will outweigh the gains and, in due course, I may become as weak and ignorant and incontinent as a newborn baby. *By the time I die much of me will already be dead,* and the "I" that dies may be a very different person from the "I" that I am now, the "I" that I was in my youth, and the "I" that I was when I was born.

We tend to assume that we have some essence or soul which is the unchanging "I". The very term *identity* is defined as "The quality of being the same; absolute or essential sameness; oneness" (*Shorter Oxford English Dictionary*). Yet, as we have seen, *human personality is constantly changing, and our sense of permanence is an illusion.* If, as many hope, the human personality survives death, which personality is this? Is it the silly old fool, the ignorant adolescent, or the newborn baby? Whatever continuity there is cannot depend on the knowledge and other brain-dependent functions that I acquire or lose in the course of my life. Similarly, common sense soon puts paid to theological arguments about the point in time when babies or embryos acquire souls, for the one thing that does seem undoubted is the fact *that each stage of our existence is a gradual process of development from the last.* In the womb, we repeat the history of our evolution from unicellular to multi-cellular aquatic creatures, from fish to reptiles to land-dwelling mammals, and, eventually, to *Homo sapiens.*

I find it more logical to believe that my present consciousness, my sense of identity, has developed gradually over time than to believe that it suddenly sprung into its present magnificent being at a particular moment in time. It seems to me quite likely that *single-celled creatures, including my own body cells, have some rudimentary kind of consciousness*—the spermatozoon, vigorously swimming to its destiny, the ciliated epithelium of my lungs, ceaselessly sweeping them clean of dust; and, most surprising of all, the lymphocyte, which responds vigorously to invasion by bacteria or other pathogens. But the lymphocyte becomes sluggish and slow in its response if I, its parent body, have suffered a bereavement, and it is tempting to suspect that it too is grieving. These creatures may not share my vision of the world, but I would be surprised if they did not have some awareness of their own existence. And if them, why not the more passive ova and the immobile cells that make up most of the body's structure?

Viewed in this way then, *I am a society*—a conglomeration of individuals who are linked together by a nervous system that gives rise to a kind of joint consciousness. Individual cells in my body are born and die, but, over a longer span of time, the body of which they are a part goes on. At a higher level, the constituents of my family and my larger society are born and die, but, over a yet longer span of time, the greater unit of which they are a part goes on. Most of us are well aware of there being something more important than us as individuals, and many of us are quite prepared to sacrifice our own lives for the preservation of that greater whole. We can accept the prospect of our own death in the hope that it will contribute to the immortality of our families, our nation, and even of humankind itself.

Thus far I may have brought my reader with me, but the next step is more speculative. It attempts to answer the question: *what happens to consciousness at the point of death*? In order to do this, it is necessary to examine the nature of the life of the cell itself. Like identity, this is usually assumed to be clear-cut: either a cell is alive or it is not, and, by implication, if the cell has some sort of rudimentary consciousness during life, that consciousness will be abruptly terminated at the moment of its death. Yet the assumption that there is an abrupt discontinuity between living and non-living substances has been thrown into doubt by recent studies. The boundary between primitive living organisms such as viruses and complex organic compounds is not clear. At that level, none of the defining characteristics of life—such as movement, growth, and reproduction—clearly distinguishes one substance from another, and *it seems likely that, in the evolution of living organisms, we are again dealing with a gradual transition rather than an abrupt discontinuity*. Again, we have to face the possibility that the rudimentary consciousness that I have postulated as existing in all living organisms has evolved gradually out of some yet more rudimentary consciousness in the complex organic compounds that preceded it, and, if in them, why not in the inorganic substances from which they too derive? While I would not argue that this "consciousness" bears much resemblance to the sophisticated awareness of self and others that is possessed by human beings, *it seems to me just as likely that there is some form of "I-ness" in all matter as that there is none*.

In evolving from organic matter into a living organism, *we build walls around ourselves*. Evolution is a process of differentiation. A group of molecules aggregate together in the primordial sea; they develop an inside and an outside. The outside is different from the inside and has to be kept out. At the cellular level, cell walls exist to separate organisms from the environment that is now external to the cell. As they move up the scale of life, multi-cellular organisms develop impervious layers of skin, exoskeletons, or other barriers to further separate them from the world outside themselves. Viewed in this way, *it is life and not death that separates us from each other*. But the more and the thicker the barriers between the units of our organization, the more difficult it is for the organism to operate as a whole. The nervous system and the organs of communication that play so large a part in linking us to our own bodies and to each other have evolved to restore communication across these boundaries. We tend to assume that our identity resides in these organs, yet I would argue that *these organs are simply ways of restoring the links that life has severed*.

When a person dies the body immediately begins to break down into its constituent organic and inorganic parts. All of the barriers break down along with the organs of communication. Nothing is lost; *everything is transmuted into another form of existence*. In that sense, at any rate, *we are all immortal*. We may not meet up with the people we love in a recognizable form and in a recognizable world, but we become one with them in much the same way that a raindrop becomes one with the pond into which it falls. And since matter is involved in a sequence of cycles in which inorganic molecules coalesce to form organic molecules, organic molecules are consumed to become living organisms and living organisms complete the cycle by dying—*so we are involved in a cycle of death and rebirth that has no predictable end*.

It is impossible for us to imagine what this transition feels like, and it seems unlikely to bear much resemblance to the popular images of the soul's passage to another world. On the other hand, it is equally fallacious to assume that we cease to be. The abiding existential nightmare of non-being makes no sense. If we are to adopt any symbolic language to describe the transition, it must be seen as movement into light rather than darkness. As Shelley (1821) put it: "Life, like a dome of many coloured glass, stains the white radiance of eternity." All we can be sure of is that our existence beyond life *will be completely different* from the life we know now.

This long diversion from the theme of this book has been necessary because of the major part that matters of life and death play in all world religions and in the confidence that we place in God. If death is the end of everything, then life loses much of its meaning and God becomes as transient as life itself. If, as I believe, we are all part of something much bigger than ourselves, some ebb and flow in the cycle of existence to which, in our lives, we each contribute something permanent and ineradicable (for good or ill), then *we are justified in regarding the spirit or essence of God as similarly transcendental.*

As to the personal view of God: *it does help if we have some image of God, some idea of a person whose hand we can hold, as we step into the dark.* If we accept that our personal view of God must be derived from the meanings that we find in life, *then God is most importantly found in the people and things that we find important, most particularly in the people we love.* When people say "God is Love", it seems to be this particular essence that they are trying to express.

And so *the wheel comes full circle* and I am back with Father God and Baby Jesus and Santa Claus and the Earth Mother and all of the myths and legends that Jung called "Archetypes" and the Ancient Greeks "The Gods". For it is not unreasonable to assume that *the spirit of God resides in all of them, however childish or silly they may seem.*

Does this theory have practical and moral implications, or is it simply an intellectual exercise, a "head trip"? I think that it does. First, it is obvious that *if God resides in the quality as well as the order of all things, then we should respect that quality.* It is not only people but other creatures and even non-living objects that deserve our attention and respect. That is not to say that all are of equal worth; we must strive to refine our own powers of judging worth and preserving and fostering it wherever we find it. A beautiful statue can be seen as resulting both from the creative imagination of the sculptor and from the interaction between the sculptor and a particular stone. Similarly, Justice results not from Law but from the interaction of a judge and a person whose behaviour has brought him or her into conflict with society; it may be helped or hindered by the Law.

We should not confuse cost with worth. The fact that caviar costs more than bread does not mean that it is worth more than bread. People and objects that are dismissed as common and cheap may be of equal or greater value than those who have achieved fame or significance because of their wealth or rarity. When my children were young and I walked them to school each day, we used to play a game called "Treasure". The children were free to pick up anything they wished—a stone, a scrap of paper, a leaf. Whatever it was became the topic of our conversation for that day. It did not take much imagination or knowledge of science to disclose the beauty and the wonders that lay in common objects. If we start with the basic assumption that all things are inherently worthwhile, we shall not go far wrong.

Second, *because each person's view of God is unique to that person, we should respect that difference*. People have a right to their own comprehension of God, and, while they have no right to interfere with ours, so we have no right to treat them or their views with disrespect. The Australian aboriginal who finds God in rocks and animals, and who, in some sense, *becomes* his totem animal when he takes part in tribal dances, is celebrating an aspect of God just as is the Christian who finds God in the bread and wine of the Eucharist.

Third, while we may need to make use of a wide range of symbols and myths to help us to think about God, we should not treat these myths as if they were literally true. If we can distinguish between the psychological truth and the literal falsity of a dream or a poem, so we should recognize that many of *the stories, anthropocentric symbols, and visual images we have of God are pointers to meaning, not truths in and of themselves*. If we do this, we may be surprised to find that we end up with a clearer view of their value. Those of us who were brought up as Christians will have a very powerful image of God as Jesus Christ, and we need to be clear in our minds that our worship of that image reflects our need to find a link with God rather than God's need to be flattered by us. As Robinson (1963) put it: "Any image can become an idol, and I believe that Christians must go through the agonizing process of detaching themselves from this idol." In doing so, they may find a richer vision of the meaning of Christ.

The concept of a multi-layered universe in which there is an ebb and flow between inorganic and organic, organic and living, cellular and individual organism, and individual organism and society, each ascending level involving a more complex organization, with those higher in the chain manipulating and controlling those elements at a lower level of organization, implies that, during our lives, we should respect and cherish those elements. *For the first time in history we have an opportunity to make links between all human beings*, and to create channels of communication and organization that transcend the tribal and national organizations that, up to now, have had to fight with each other in order to survive.

For a long time now we have been able to share knowledge across such boundaries, and modern methods of communication are bringing about the new level of "cooperative interthinking" or corporate identity which comes close to being what Huxley (1964) termed "the equivalent of a person". While it is difficult to imagine how this "person" could develop any sort of consciousness independent of the individuals who make it up, the sharing of a consensus view of the world already moves us in that direction. If spouses or partners can come to see themselves as "one person" as they share more and more assumptions about the world, and if members of traditional families can be so firmly attached that they are willing to sacrifice their lives for each other, so the "global village"—which includes popular "soaps" and "chat" shows as well as news broadcasts and the Internet—bids fair to replace the traditional family. It may well turn out to be an extremely potent source of identity for future generations.

We are right to be anxious about this phenomenon, for those who control its content carry great responsibility though they do not always show it. I have no doubt that it will influence the image that young people have of God, who may well end up looking more like Luke Skywalker than the old man on the ceiling of the Sistine chapel. In the meanwhile, *the preservation of all that is sacred, just, beautiful, and/or worthy of respect is a reasonable aim and likely to reflect the spirit of God.*

CHAPTER TEN

Freud, feminism, and religion

Janet Sayers

Freud famously regarded religion as an illusion. He implied that it was akin to the dreams and nightmares that are the stuff of psychoanalysis. As such, religion, like our sleeping fantasies, draws both on the realities of our waking life and on those created from the dynamic of the unconscious and conscious, spiritual and secular, psychic and material realities of our inner and outer worlds. At least this is my view, as I will seek to explain in this chapter through a dream that I relate towards the end, and through recounting and illustrating the theories of psychoanalysis and feminism informing my work as a Freudian therapist, but beginning with a brief autobiographical account of the place of religion in my life.

Autobiography

My mother is Jewish. But my grandfather's and father's nonconformist, fundamentalist Plymouth Brethren and Baptist theologies were the major determinant of my childhood religious belief. I experienced their Christianity, in its certainties, as simultaneously comforting and confining, just as others recount, in feminist and Freudian terms, a similar contradiction in the certainties of Jewish fundamentalism and patriarchal authoritarianism as a defence against the anxiety of post-modern uncertainty (e.g. Frosh, 1997).

I remember an incident when, aged 5 or 6 years, I felt torn between the comforting Sunday routine of going to church and dreading being confined by the church doors closing on me. I remember this contradiction in terms of the stomach cramps that then assailed me, and the fear of mentioning them lest my father angrily interpret such talk as an excuse invented to get out of going to morning service. I remember similar conflicts in my early teens. I remember dithering whether to take issue with my father about his injunction that I, as a girl and unlike the men in my family, must wear a hat in church. I remember my hesitancy whether to admit to him my fears about believing, as he did, in life after death.

Most of all, however, I remember religious arguments with two women in secondary school, leading me to share my mother's pantheistic agnosticism. As though these women were two divided aspects of myself, I recall deriding one and revering the other. On the one hand, I derided the first woman, the headmistress of my church grammar school, as a fool for greeting my resistance to getting baptised or confirmed like my fellow-pupils on the grounds that I did not believe in God by recommending that I pray to God for belief. Since I did not believe in Him, I reasoned, her recommendation was absurd. There was no way that, not believing in God, I could address let alone pray to Him. On the other hand, I thought very highly of my next headmistress at the progressive school that I attended after leaving grammar school. Unlike her predecessor, she took on board, thought about, and countered what I had to say about my then religious belief, not so much in God as about an after-life of fire and brimstone, hell and damnation.

Her thoughtful and critical attention and understanding, analogous to the attitude that, according to Freud, it behoves analysts to adopt with their patients, doubtless contributed both to the development of my subsequent disbelief in Christianity and to my developing an image of the after-life not as a terrifying inferno but as one of reassuring psychic and spiritual communion with others. I had a particularly vivid experience of this one day in my mid-teens when, walking through an azalea grove near a church-yard rumoured to be haunted by a grey lady, I felt filled with an uplifting sense of community with all who had gone before me, past and present, living and dead. Perhaps it was also my second secondary-school headmistress's understanding that contributed to my current willingness to share with my father's family the reassurance that they derive at family funerals from believing that the death of our relatives signifies their transition to a happier world than this.

I accordingly remain irritated by the memory of a supervisor at Cambridge who, evincing none of the empathy or understanding of my headmistress, and who, despite his supervising me for a degree in Moral Sciences, assumed that since I was studying philosophy, I, like him, could not believe in God. I was much more favourably inclined to the teaching of another lecturer, John Wisdom. He likened belief in God to belief that the healthy growth of plants in an otherwise withering garden is due to the work of an unseen gardener (Wisdom, 1944). He compared belief in God to belief in the unconscious, and he likened both beliefs to seeing a snake in the grass after first interpreting signs of its presence in other, non-serpentine terms (Wisdom, 1950).

Wisdom's teaching undoubtedly contributed to my deciding, after leaving Cambridge, to train as a Clinical Psychologist at the Tavistock Clinic in London. There I learnt a version of psychoanalysis which was entirely compatible with the pantheistic creed of oneness and connection with others in which, like my mother, I had by then come to believe. I became steeped at the Tavistock not in Freud's father-centred theory of psychoanalysis and religion in which Freud conceptualized the psyche, in individualistic terms, as essentially disconnected from others; rather, I learnt the psychoanalytic theories of our interpersonal connectedness with others advanced not only by Klein and Winnicott, but also in lectures at the clinic by Bowlby on attachment theory and by Laing on the dialectic of our being-for-ourselves and our being-for-others.

All that now remains of the God-fearing faith I imbibed from my grandfather's and father's Christianity is its symbols of which

I am repeatedly reminded in Canterbury where my husband and I have lived since 1970. I recall one of the first patients I assessed in St Augustine's Hospital, which was named after the man who in AD 597 first officially brought Christianity from Rome to Canterbury. My patient was a stonemason at the Cathedral, and I recall thinking of him then, as I think of him now, in terms of the symbolism of the religiously tormented hero of Thomas Hardy's novel *Jude the Obscure*.

Through the 1970s and 1980s I was moved each year, especially the Christmas that our first son was born, by the regalia of the Cathedral's Advent procession. But then, belatedly, I read Virginia Woolf's book *Three Guineas*. In it Woolf drew attention to the harm done to women in the name of the patriarchal, phallic even, insignia of England's church and state. She illustrated her thesis with photographs of a general in his cockaded helmet, royal heralds with their trumpets, university dignitaries with a mace, ending with a photograph of the archbishop with his mitre and crook.

Reading Woolf's book marked yet another watershed in my religious belief, for I read it after having spent a decade becoming increasingly involved, both politically and in my teaching and research after becoming a lecturer at the University of Kent in 1974, in the feminist struggle to right the wrongs done women by the patriarchy that Woolf so well documented. The 1970s saw the heyday of understanding these wrongs as an effect of patriarchy's "ideological state apparatuses", as recounted by the philosopher Louis Althusser (1971) in terms of the theories of Marx and Freud.

Theory

Particularly important as regards the women's movement was Juliet Mitchell's (1974) account of the version of psychoanalysis on which Althusser drew, namely that developed by Jacques Lacan. She urged the relevance for feminism of Freud's work, at least as interpreted by Lacan, in so far as Freud's theory of the Oedipus and castration complex explains both sexes' unconscious fantasy, from early childhood, of the father as quasi-god or superego. Psychoanalysis, according to Mitchell, thereby explains both sexes' initiation, via the unconscious, into patriarchy and its symbolism including, most of all, its symbol of man as patriarch or phallic god.

Subsequently other feminist theorists have gone along with both Freud's and Lacan's more or less explicit claim that God is the symbol of our looking to our fathers for protection and refuge from the helplessness and risk of psychosis involved in the variously self-aggrandizing and self-annihilating delusion of being fused with the mother of our infancy (as I explain at greater length in Sayers, 1995). Feminists have taken issue with the "master discourse" of Enlightenment philosophy—including the father-centred "modernist" discourses of Freudian and Lacanian psychoanalysis. They have instead insisted that we are not produced by a single discourse. Rather, they argue that we are produced as sexed subjects by a multiplicity of different discourses (e.g. Chodorow, 1994) including those of religion and psychoanalysis.

Still others counter the patriarchalism of psychoanalysis by drawing on often religiously informed, mother-centred symbols and motifs. Some counter the religious myths and legends of men as gods and heroes researched by Jung in developing his analytical psychology theory of the collective unconscious and its archetypes with myths and legends of women as goddesses and heroines (e.g. Bolen, 1992; Estes, 1992; Goodison, 1990).

Meanwhile, many Freudian feminists counter Freud's patriarchal individualism with a mother-based version of psychoanalysis stressing our connection with others, just as Romain Rolland long ago countered Freud's father-based account of religion by stressing the religious sentiment involved in "a feeling as of something limitless, unbounded, as it were 'oceanic'" (Freud, 1930a, p. 251). Freud likened this feeling to our sense of boundless oneness with our mothers as babies. Feminists often pursue a similar tack. Adopting the mother-based theory advanced by the sociologist, now psychoanalyst, Nancy Chodorow (1978), they often draw on the version of psychoanalysis developed by Winnicott. He described religion as a transitional object created, like other transitional objects, to bridge the gap between the inner reality of our subjective fusion or "oceanic" unity with others, in the first place with our mothers, and the outer reality of our objective separateness and difference, as individuals, from them (e.g. Winnicott, 1953; Wulff, 1997).

These formulations as forwarded by feminism, however, often overlook the divisions of love and hate involved in our sense of fusion and connection with others. This includes, in the case of analysis, the relation of analyst and analysand which Klein (1946) and her followers theorized as involving projective identification, maternal reverie, and containment (e.g. Bion, 1962).

An exception to the general oversight by feminists of the divisions in women's closeness with each other, in the first place with their mothers, is the work of the feminist psychologist Dorothy Dinnerstein (1976). Drawing on Klein's theories, Dinnerstein claims that both sexes avoid the guilt and depression involved in facing and bringing these divisions together by escaping them for the unrealistic solace of idealizing and idolizing men. Because of continuing inequalities in childcare, and because of men's relative absence from children's early lives, Dinnerstein maintains that men are particularly likely to be idealized and idolized as an escape from the fantasies of love and hate with which we endow the women who first mother us. Or, as Klein (e.g. 1928, 1957) put it, boys often find refuge from nightmare ambivalence about their mothers in celebrating their masculinity, their having a penis, while girls often find refuge in shifting their love, affection, and desire from the mother to the father and to other men in his stead.

But flight into idolizing men and masculinity does nothing to address or integrate the divisions of love and hate, envy and gratitude, impelling this hoped-for escape. These divisions remain to plague the very idolization looked to as refuge from them. Hence the ills done by the idolizing or idealizing fantasy of the parents as superego figures—all too often reinforced by religious idealization of fathers and mothers as gods and goddesses—that is so often a major source, according to Freudian and Kleinian theory, of the suffering bringing women and men into analysis. Far from bolstering these deities, the solution, psychoanalytically, lies in confronting and working to bring together our love and hate of those to whom we are physically, emotionally, and spiritually closest on a more realistic, less escapist basis.

I have sketchily illustrated this process in recounting the shift in my religious belief in God, through division in my attitudes to my secondary school headmistresses, to belief in spiritual or at least psychological connection with others, with all the divided feelings that this involves. In the following sections of this chapter, I illustrate similar shifts occurring in patients with whom I have worked in the NHS as a clinical psychologist. I recount here three examples (in which I have changed all identifying details) that all involve religious motifs (cf. Jones, 1991). They centre on depression, loneliness, and group analysis, respectively.

Depression

I will begin with depression, specifically with the depression of a woman whom I will call Charlotte. Charlotte was in her late 50s when she first came for once-weekly individual psychotherapy. She began by telling me how ashamed she was of herself. Her husband had left her many years ago because she was no good in bed. She had never got another man. Her son—largely through her incompetence as a mother, she told me—was a failure. Her body was lopsided. Anaemia prevented her from ever completing her training as an opera singer. Part-time work scarcely earned her any money. She was impoverished. And she was so incapable of following the diet prescribed her on account of her diabetes that she was already suffering its legacy of debilitating headaches and would soon be crippled with arthritis and blindness as well. She was "on the scrap-heap", she told me, with "nowhere to go but down".

Telling me her sorry tale, it emerged from occasional hints she let slip about the shortcomings of her father and ex-husband that occasionally, albeit fleetingly, she felt disappointed in and aggrieved at them. More often, however, like the depressed housewife described by Freud (1917e)—who defends against disappointment in her husband by deifying, internalizing, and identifying with him as an ideal figure and berates herself, not him, for falling short of the ideals with which she bestows him—Charlotte berated herself. This included berating herself for not living up to the ideals of "the good life" preached, she told me, by the English statesman, Catholic martyr, and saint, Thomas More, whose head is said to be buried in Canterbury.

She was disappointed in herself. She was also disappointed in being allocated me as her therapist—a woman whom she experienced as being as deficient as she experienced herself. She wished she could have been allocated a man, the consultant psychiatrist who first assessed her on her referral to the clinic, as her therapist. Her disappointment in me, like her depressed disappointment in herself, was fuelled by angry memories of her mother, who had died a couple of years before she started therapy. She complained that her mother, together with her father, had let her down as a child. Her parents, she said, had never recognized her uniqueness. They had treated her and her siblings all scrupulously the same without any regard for their individual differences from each other. She complained that they had never noticed or applauded her achievements as a child or adult, just as she feared I too might not acknowledge or applaud her being different to and more accomplished than my other patients.

For want of her parents' and my applause, she applauded herself. She boasted her erudition and superiority by quoting recondite snatches from opera arias. She boasted her religious awe and oneness with the God-soaring heights of Canterbury's towering Cathedral. She boasted her pantheistic oneness with nature. She contrasted her spirituality with the petty-mindedness of her neighbours cutting down the buttercups and daisies in their lawns in obsessively mowing them each week, just as I was petty-minded and obsessively even-handed in the weekly routine of psychotherapy I doled out to her.

In this state of mind, she was like those whom the Kleinian analyst Henri Rey (1977) characterizes as fleeing the guilt and depression involved in bringing together, integrating, and working to repair the damage done to love by hate by imagining themselves to be God-like above all such pettiness. Rey illustrates the point in terms of a patient who symbolized this high-and-mighty state of mind in terms of a dream in which he had a magic wand—a long penis-like pole—reaching to the sky on the end of his nose.

As for Charlotte, her oscillation between imagining herself as high above it all—close to God—and hating herself for being nothing of the kind gradually gave way to another calmer state of mind. She expressed this mood too in religious terms. She talked of her growing love for and attachment to her daughter's mother-in-law, Kate. She talked of her pleasure in their shared belief in God. She likened the inspiration she derived from her new-found friendship to the inspiration she derived from a Renaissance painting of the Madonna, a reproduction of which hung over her bed at home. She brought the picture to one of her therapy sessions for me to see. She recounted her pleasure in going with Kate on religious retreat to a convent, and the peace of mind she gained from reading the religious texts that Kate recommended to her.

It was therefore a bitter blow when, towards the end of therapy, she learnt that Kate had cancer. But she also greeted the news of her friend's anticipated death with relative equanimity. Perhaps her calm was a measure not only of the peace that she derived from her shared faith with her friend in God, but also of feeling less divided by feelings of grievance and superiority towards me from shared faith in and commitment to our joint work in her therapy.

Loneliness

By contrast, Frances, also divorced and in her 50s when she came for therapy, retained to the end of our sessions together a less oscillating, more self-satisfied mood of obedience to God and to the dictates both of her Catholic religion and of therapy. She came for help fearful of the loneliness that she dreaded would befall her when her youngest child, who had just completed her A-levels, left home for college.

Whereas Charlotte had played down the shortcomings of her father and ex-husband, Frances played up those of the men in her life. She hated her father, she told me. She had no love for him. She was revolted by him. She was disgusted by a childhood memory of seeing him playing sexually with himself. She had been reminded of this memory later when a man sexually exposed himself to her on a bus. She hated her father's preoccupation with himself. She hated his lack of interest in, and lack of consideration for, her. She contrasted her religious obedience and her regular church attendance with his irregularity—with the in-continence of his sexuality and with the incontinence of his incipient dementia in not organizing himself regularly to attend the meals provided by his local day centre.

It was the same with her ex-husband. She hated and despised him for his lack of self-discipline, for his scurrilously breaching the stipulations of their Catholic religion against adultery and divorce in leaving her some years before for another woman to whom he was now married. She was determined to show him up, to parade his sins and inadequacies compared to her religious conformity, faith, zeal, and obedience. That was why, it transpired, she was so insistent on telling herself and me that, unlike her husband, and true to the rules of their church, she would never re-marry nor have sex with anyone else. That was why the only men with whom she was friends were priests bound by rules of chastity and celibacy from marrying or having sex with her.

Her conformity with the strictures of her religion, like her conformity with the strictures of therapy—in obediently attending her sessions with me each week and in obediently telling me all about herself—was a means, it turned out, of avenging herself on her father and husband. In thus expressing her hatred of them, her self-righteous piety and dutifulness did nothing to dispel or mitigate her hatred with love.

Just as she continued to hate them, she felt similarly negative towards a priest to whom she had recently looked for comfort. She scorned him for being too weak to deal with the feelings evoked in him by her wanting to confide her personal troubles to him. She scorned him for defensively reacting by cutting her off from God, as she put it, by enjoining her to confide not in him but me.

Her religiosity did nothing to allay these images of others as contemptible, hated, and despised. They remained in her mind to haunt and plague her from within when she was by herself. Hence her dread of being alone, in keeping with both Freudian and Jungian observations on the inner representation of our relations with others as loved or hated which variously render solitude a peaceful heaven or a warlike hell (e.g. Klein, 1963; Storr, 1989; Winnicott, 1958).

Therapy accordingly became a matter of confronting and integrating her splitting of love from hate on a more sound and genuine basis than was afforded by her sanctimonious, genuflecting, worshipful obedience to the God and regulations of her church. In particular, it involved reworking this split, as she vehemently expressed it, in the love and hate of her two daughters who, it became apparent, represented two unreconciled aspects of herself experienced in terms of her religion as sacred and profane.

Group analysis

My third example bears on a similar division. It is drawn from the fifth and last meeting before Christmas of a therapy group—consisting of Sally, Sarah, Diane, Bernice, Polly, Keith, and Tom—which I was then running with a colleague, David. The session began in silence, broken by Sally and Tom trying to get a conversation going about the ups and downs of being with their children.

Sally bemoaned the fact that whatever she did to help her 10-year-old son with his schoolwork, and whatever she did to tidy up and decorate the Christmas tree at home, nothing did any good. Her son criticized her housekeeping. He hated her. She hated herself for hating him. It got her down, she said, as her children and everyone else could see from the dismal black clothes she wore day in, day out. She dejectedly went on to recount how, despite always feeding her children nourishing, additive-free food—unlike the junk she fed herself—other children with their diet of crisps and pop were evidently much healthier than her children and herself.

At this point, Tom took up Sally's talk of the perils and rewards of childcare. He told her that being careful about what her children ate made her better than other children's mothers. He recounted being divided, like her, as regards childcare. He recounted being divided between indulgence and control in looking after his 3-year-old son. He talked of attending his son's playgroup Christmas party the day before. He talked of how, unlike the other children, who had eaten nutritious sandwiches at the party, his son had eaten through a pile of marshmallows. Half an hour later, as a result of all the sugar he had fed himself, said Tom, his son became impossibly hyperactive, naughty, and unmanageable. So, Tom said, he stopped his son eating for several hours "to get rid of the poisons from his body". Only then was his son hungry enough to take in the mixed blessings of something solid and substantial—potatoes and swede. "Well", Tom added, "Not the swede. But he did eat the potatoes."

The group, however, was in no mood for talk of the divisions of what is wanted and not wanted, of good and bad in feeding, of looking after and of being with others. Nor was the group in any mood to pursue Tom's subsequent talk—after I had drawn attention to the distress of another member, Polly, who had been crying since the session began—of sometimes having, as Tom put it, "to go down into the shit" and "look inside oneself for inner strength". The group was in no mood for thinking about an inner world of strength and weakness, good and bad, stagnation and change. In a previous session, Tom had formulated this last division in terms of the change wrought in his life when, after years of alcoholism, he contracted a life-threatening illness. It was God working within him, he said, telling him he must give up drink, develop, and grow.

Not heeding the presence of God, as Tom said he had done, the group was not in Christmas but Good Friday mood. The group was in the mood represented in the Bible by the image of Christ on the cross beseeching his father in heaven—"My God, my God, why has thou forsaken me?" (Matthew 27: 46). The group was intent on indulging the misery of the absence of its god or leader—my colleague David, whom they had been warned some weeks before would unfortunately not be able to attend this session. The group members' dedication to feeling woefully bereft became apparent in the rapt attention, in contrast to its shuffling disinterest in Tom's and Sally's childcare conversation, with which they greeted the woeful tales of being forsaken by their men with which Polly and Sarah now regaled the group.

Recovering from her tears, Polly explained that her upset was due to her boyfriend having left her that week for a former girlfriend who had returned to be looked after by him over Christmas. Sally pointed out that Polly had other friends she could turn to and be with. But Polly and other group members would have no truck with talk of substitutes, just as they made it clear that I was no substitute for their leader, David, being away. They wanted to hear tales of being forsaken, now recounted by Polly likening her lover's infidelity to all the other "abandonments", as she put it, that she had suffered since she was a 2-year-old: never knowing her father; not being there when he died; and, after fifteen years of marriage, being abandoned by her husband leaving her for another woman from one week to the next.

When I suggested that the spellbinding effect of Polly's story was due to it mirroring the group's feeling of being abandoned from one week to the next by its leader David, and by the prospect of being abandoned by both of us as its leaders over the next two weeks' Christmas break, Sarah proved the point by capping Polly's story. She mesmerized the group with yet another tale of abandonment, of being abandoned by her husband. She depicted him in quasi-religious terms as a spiritually inspired ascetic. She recounted how six years before, in the name of giving up all his worldly goods, he had got rid of his business, everything they owned, all his possessions—including her—and left for a monastic existence. He continued to live on his own, she told the group, with only his music for company and inspiration.

Later in the session, Sally tried to rally the group with talk of hands-on massage therapy. But the group persisted in its sense of being forsaken by its absent, hands-off, "talk therapy" leader. Its mood remained that characterized by the Kleinian analyst Wilfred Bion (1961) and also discussed in a religious context by the group analyst Earl Hopper (1988). The group's mood remained one of defending against its reality-oriented or ego-oriented work—in this instance, the work proposed by Sally and Tom of facing and resolving the divisions involved in their togetherness and connection with others as parents and children—by instead taking refuge in the "basic assumption" fantasy, as Bion put it, of meeting together to depend on a shared leader, elevated to the status of god, without whom nothing can be done but grieve.

Fact and Fiction

Through the above anecdotes and examples, I have sought to illustrate how I draw on Freudian and feminist theory in understanding Christian iconography as symbolic of fluctuations in
both my own and my patients' minds between acknowledging
and fleeing to god-like figures from the divisions involved in our
physical, emotional, and spiritual closeness to and connection
with others. I will end with one last example to highlight the contradiction between fact and fiction in the images furnished by external reality—including the reality of organized religion—informing our dreams and nightmares, which, as I observed at the
beginning of this chapter, are the stuff of psychoanalysis.

My example concerns a dream I had one night when I was
working on this piece. Jack, an erstwhile academic colleague of
whose death I had been reminded the day before, was involved
in the dream. Previously I had learnt that Jack had died of an
illness resulting from his having not one but several spleens (possibly due to his father having been irradiated by nuclear testing
before Jack was conceived). Following my dream, I likened Jack's
condition to cats proverbially having not one but nine lives.

In my dream, Jack was alive. He was a doctor. He talked to me
about three other people at the party that we were attending. They were
dead. But they were standing upright, swaddled in white bandages like
Egyptian mummies. Jack told me that in order for our fellow-guests to
die, actually and in fact, all three would have to be pierced at the side of
their lips so as to briefly revive them by letting their blood out of
their bodies. Only then, Jack said, could they finally and absolutely die.
So saying he started piercing them. Blood began seeping and oozing
red through the whiteness of their winding sheets. At this I woke up,
terrified of falling asleep again lest this nightmare image recur
and again live in my mind.

Reflecting on this experience, I realize just how much my
childhood and early teenage religious belief was less about God
than about the after-life. My dream, however, also illustrates the
way that we draw on both factual and fanciful images in external
reality as a means of representing symbolically and metaphorically the psychic reality of our inner world.

In my dream, I drew both on the truth of Jack having several spleens and on the untruth that cats have nine lives. I drew on the fact that the ancient Egyptians mummified their dead and on the fantasy that through mummifying them they could ensure the dead continuing life. My dream also drew on the only images available to us of being dead (cf. Rose, 1993), namely those drawn from the facts and fantasies informing our experience of being alive—including the image of a living and animate body inside an inanimate shroud.

I also drew on the fictional motif, arguably informed by the image of blood signifying death and by the image of sexual penetration and breast-feeding signifying life, of the vampire both killing and conferring immortality on his victims by piercing, biting, sucking, and letting their blood. As far as Christian cosmology is concerned, my dream led me to think of reincarnation, an idea reiterated in the Bible and also repressed as Gnostic heresy—as an "anathema"—by Constantine when he established Christianity as approved religion in ancient Rome. My dream also led to thoughts of the New Testament story of Christ's death and resurrection.

Conclusion

I began this chapter with Freud's famous, or infamous, account of religion as an illusion. He was also infamously cavalier about the facts, as opposed to the fantasies, determining his patients' psychology. Feminists have repeatedly criticized his work on this account. They have again and again taken issue with psychoanalysis for the wrongs done women by Freud's abandonment of his "seduction theory" in favour of the view that his women patients' hysteria was more an effect of imagined than of actual abuse, and by Freud's characterization of women's protest about their lot as an effect of fantasy-ridden penis envy.

By combining feminism and psychoanalysis, I have sought to recount and explain my own and my patients' oscillation between belief in God and belief in community with others, including struggling with the divisions of love and hate involved. However, learning from Freud, I hope I do not similarly wrong my patients in understanding their religion—at least the God of Christianity—as more fantasy than fact, as a metaphor on which I and they draw in externalizing so as to share and think with others about our inner world.

CHAPTER ELEVEN

Religion and science in psychoanalysis

Neville Symington

There is, I believe, a crisis within psychoanalysis and within the psychotherapy schools that derive from it. Hardly a week goes by when our enemies do not assail us in the media. This is healthy. Criticism and challenge can only sharpen our minds to think more clearly and reflect more deeply upon our practice and its methods. What worries me is the replies to these taunts from our own practitioners rushing, as we usually do, to our own defence. Many of these criticisms are prejudiced assaults that do not deserve much attention, but there is a common theme running through much of the critique which has some basis. It is that the "talking cure", as it was called by Freud, is not producing any result; that patients visit their analyst or therapist year in, year out, with no visible change in their condition. Now I know that this is a sweeping generalization that does not apply across the board, but one thing I do know is that it is often the case. I have heard clinical presentations where a patient has been visit-

---

This chapter is an adaptation of a lecture given at the Freud Conference in Melbourne, Australia, on 2 April 1995.

ing an analyst or therapist for four, five, six, even ten years without any change that I was able to detect. I have not heard this on just isolated occasions but frequently. These are the obvious cases where no change has occurred and what one might call a malingering situation has set in. But even in cases where it looks as though change has occurred, it is often a case of subtle accommodation to the analyst or therapist, and the patient remains with the same mental structure within. Most frequently this consists of a mentality that is paranoid. I am not here supporting many of the burgeoning therapies that claim to cure mental disturbance in a much quicker, efficient, and cost-effective way. Many of these therapies only give the appearance of cure. The criterion used to measure success is often simply a patient who "feels cured" or who "feels better". However, experienced clinicians know that such feelings are an insufficient criterion. We have all seen the cases where such a statement is made with confidence one day and the next day the person has committed suicide. No, I am not criticizing psychoanalysis alone but the whole psychotherapy movement. In fact, I believe that, within a sick situation, psychoanalysis is probably the healthiest patient. So if my remarks in this paper apply to psychoanalysis, they apply *a fortiori* all the more so to the enormous array of therapies that bloom so luxuriantly in present-day Western society.

Let me start with the hypothesis that there is something wrong, that there is something rotten in the state of Denmark. What is its cause? I believe that it is twofold: that psychoanalysis is both failing to be scientific and failing to be religious. Unless these two axes transect the process, the analytic experience remains sterile. I must now try to explain what I mean.

I said that the patient remains with an inner paranoia, and, if you detected in that statement a pejorative judgement, you would be correct. Wherein lies the source of this judgement? What is wrong with a mentality that is paranoid? Why should anyone impugn me for having it? There was a time when I tried to argue that paranoia was repugnant to the survival instinct. I remember lecturing at the Tavistock Clinic in London where I gave as a lucid exemplar Burke, of the fateful Burke and Wills expedition. As some of you may know, this was an expedition mounted in the latter half of the last century to explore the central part of

Australia, which at that time was unknown. When Burke was weak and starving in that desert land, in the region of Cooper's Creek, the aborigines came creeping towards his camp. In a burst of paranoid passion, Burke started firing his revolver furiously at them, whereupon those natives wisely rescinded their friendly intent and fled away. So, said the emboldened lecturer, here is proof that paranoia is antagonistic to the survival instinct. Had Burke like King (the sole survivor of the expedition), I said, given friendly welcome to his timid visitors they would have saved his life. Yet however nice this sounds, it is pure rubbish (yet not one soul treated to this tale of high romance raised a hand in protest). Many a time has paranoia bluffed someone through the threatening interstices of life, whereas the person who has substituted paranoia with concern has perished for his pains. In my book *Emotion and Spirit* (1994), I put forward the thesis that in *mature religion* there is something more important than survival which motivates the individual.

So on what basis do I judge paranoia unfavourably? When I make this judgement, it is in terms of some criterion by which I judge it. But what is it? You will note that I have been trying to do this on the basis of the survival instinct but that it is untenable as a criterion. So what is the criterion by which paranoia is judged unfavourably? I have only plucked out paranoia as one example, but the same applies if we take sadism, masochism, or omnipotence. We all see these as being pathological, but, again, on what criterion do we make such a judgement? To try to find the answer to this question, I want to examine the role of omnipotence in mental life.

It can come as a shock to realize that a patient has entirely obliterated something in his or her perceptual field. In my consulting-room, I have a very large painting on the wall that is parallel to the couch. As a patient gets off the couch, he or she has to walk about twenty feet straight in the direction of the painting before coming to the door through to leave the consulting-room. I had been seeing a particular patient for two and a half years when, on entering the room, his head jinked towards the painting and, as he lay down, he said—"That's new, isn't it? I've never seen it before."

For two and a half years he had totally blotted the painting from his field of vision. It was a case of negative hallucination. It emerged in the analysis that this painting represented myself as a person with a free life of my own, independent from him and also his own emotional centre. Both of these were blotted out. But how is someone, such as this man, able to blot out the presence of the other so effectively? My observation tells me that it is through the presence of omnipotence. In an omnipotent state, this man was able to blot out the faculty of perception. This is the way omnipotence functions. Omnipotence, closely allied to the superego, issues instructions that are then obeyed: "Thou shalt not see the picture on the wall. If thou darest raise thine eyes and see, thou shalt be struck dead."

Wherewith cometh this omnipotent power? To answer this, I resort to another clinical vignette. A patient complained bitterly that his father was very authoritarian and then went on to say that his secretary at work would not carry out his orders. The analyst pointed out that it was he who was authoritarian and gave further evidence of this assertion, whereupon the patient went into a massive depression.

It became clear that his controlling authoritarian manner had been used to ward off a depression that the personality was not capable of managing. It was similar with the man who blotted out my painting. He consented to the situation to protect himself from a depression that he was not able to sustain. So there is an agreement within the personality to invest this figure with the power to blot out the perceptual faculty. My observation tells me that this obliteration is only possible through the agency of omnipotence. I believe that the divine figure in religious myths who turns Lot's wife into a pillar of salt or causes Eurydice to vanish into Hades is an externalization of this inner reality which has power to obliterate our mental faculties.

Now this begins to make a bit more sense of why psychoanalysis sets out to tackle the presence of omnipotence in the personality. As we have seen, it may function to protect the personality from a severe depression, but this is at the price of destroying the mental faculties. As psychoanalysis is concerned with mental development and the restoration of damaged faculties, it has the

task of integrating omnipotence so that it does not act destruc-
tively. The way that this process is integrated has been well described in a paper entitled "The Survival Function of Primitive
Omnipotence", by Joan Symington (1985). Omnipotence does not
disappear but becomes the servant of the ego rather than the
other way around. We can see from this, therefore, that psychoanalysis sets out to demote omnipotent functioning within the
personality and replace it with a form of functioning that makes
full use of available mental faculties. A person can manage by the
use of omnipotence, but only at the cost of damage to his or her
perceptual and cognitive faculties.

The cardinal sin in religious practice and devotion is pride
in the Christian tradition, *hubris* in classical thinking, or *mana* in
Buddhist practice. These words are equivalents of omnipotence or
grandiosity. Within the Judaeo–Christian tradition, this pride is
simply condemned as bad with no reason for it. Within Buddhism, it can be understood to stand in the way of reaching *nir-
vana* as it is an aspect of *dukkha*. However, through psychoanalytic
investigation, we discover that omnipotence destroys those mental faculties that are capable of revealing our inner psychic condition. We understand, therefore, that psychoanalysis aims to
transform omnipotence so that it no longer has the power to act
against the mental faculties.

However, I cannot put a full-stop there. I still have a question
to answer: why does psychoanalysis set itself this task? To answer
it, I have to examine more closely the mental faculties that are
attacked by that omnipotent part of the self. I shall go back to the
man who mentally blotted out the large painting on my wall.
Effacing that painting from his mind represented his obliteration
of myself as a separate person. This was done through deleting
part of the perceptual faculty. In the case of the painting it was
vision that was interfered with, but by what faculty is it that I
apprehend another human being as a person?

It is common for us to hear someone complaining that he or
she has been treated as a mere object by another. The other who
has perpetrated this behaviour is often quite unaware of it, just as
my patient was unaware of the presence of the large painting on
my wall. It is not perception or memory that is blotted out here
but the epistemological faculty. I apprehend another person not

though the senses but through knowledge. The person of the other is apprehended through an act of knowledge. I see a face and legs, hear a voice, smell perspiration, touch hairy skin, but have no knowledge of a person.

When I say that I know a person, is there a synonym for person? What do I mean when I say it? What am I referring to? I am, I believe, referring to the *being* of the other, and ontological reflection tells me that *being* is one and indivisible. It is therefore the reality in which I and the other share, and is the root upon which the concept of transference is based. The patient who blotted out my painting, who eradicated my personhood, also obliterated his own person. This *being* is identical with that reality apprehended by the seers whose metaphysical insights have been recorded in the Upanishads.

This radical obliteration of our *being* is the source of neurosis, psychosis, addiction, perversion, and psychopathy. The uncovering of the processes that lead to this obliteration is then *the* psychoanalytic task. Observing and cataloguing these processes in their intricacy, their subtlety, and their complexity is the scientific activity *within* psychoanalysis. It is the scientific activity *of* psychoanalysis. I will go so far as to say that the criterion of whether a technique or theory is truly psychoanalytic is whether it can be registered meaningfully within this straightforward schema. Contrariwise, all those theories and procedures that cannot be so accommodated are mere dross, only worthy of the dustbin. I believe that if this criterion were strictly followed by the editors of our professional journals and books, a veritable forest of trees would still be standing unmolested upon our landscape.

We need to stop for a moment to reflect on *being* and its nature. A human being, a plant, a stone, a dream, friendship, and the universe are objects that have an element in common: they all exist. Existence is their common denominator. Also all parts of myself exist. When I reflect on the fact that I exist, I realize that I share this with you. My existence, my *being*, is not *mine*, because once you reflect upon it you discover that it is indivisible. This is why the seers of the Upanishads, having reflected long and deeply upon this, formulated that time-honoured phrase,

THAT THOU ART.

This is a realization that does not come about through a quick piece of reasoning. In the same way as I may only realize my vulnerability and dependence after several years of analysis, so also the realization THAT THOU ART was only arrived at after concentrated reflection. It is a piece of intellectual understanding but also emotional. Many years ago I studied ontology, the science of being, under the tutelage of a philosopher who only taught what he had personally assimilated. With his help, I achieved some insight into existence. I believe that it has been the most important realization of my life. I have not achieved it as deeply as the seers of the Upanishads, nor have I been faithful to it through all the upheavals of life, but it gave me a glimpse of their vision and what it was all about. I shall refer to this reality for the rest of this chapter as our *participated being*. (*Participated being* is synonymous with *being*, but the former accents the fact that our *being* is a shared *being*.)

So, obliteration of *participated being* is the source of neurosis, psychosis, perversion, psychopathy, and personality disorder and contrariwise, the unimpeded access to *participated being* is the source of mental health and well-being. Our logical conclusion is that the person who is able to be in relation to *participated being* enjoys mental health and keeps a pathway open to ongoing emotional development.

Participated being does not lie fallow within the personality but exacts an influence. Like all parts of the personality, it is emotionally active. But what are its signals? How do we make contact with its presence? The earth's core lies 3,500 miles into its centre, but geologists tell us that it makes its presence felt at the surface through radiation waves that are responsible, together with particles from the sun, for the phenomenon of *aurora borealis*. It is also believed that the electrical currents it generates are responsible for the magnetism registered on the dial of a compass. In a similar way, there is a signal from *participated being*: we call it conscience. Now we need to spend a little time on conscience.

It is often thought that conscience speaks when I am about to injure my neighbour. It often does speak on such an occasion, but hurting my neighbour is not the reason. If the latter were the case, then dentists would be the most conscience-ridden people in our community. Analysts also often say things that hurt, and, in fact, that meddlesome conscience might start clamouring if I desist from an interpretation for fear of hurting my patient. I suspect that if a dentist were afraid to drill a tooth because of the pain he would inflict, then again that troubling voice might start to clamour. No, conscience speaks when, wielding an axe, I am about to hack and smash at *participated being*. If I do so, it will affect my neighbours, most especially those who are close to me, but that is a consequence of what I do and not the essence of it. *Participated being* makes demands upon the personality. Just as I experience hunger when the organism needs some more stored energy, so conscience clamours when *participated being* is under threat.

I once came across a criminal who had bashed an old lady over the head. About two weeks prior to this event, a forensic psychiatrist had lent him two pounds. Subsequently the criminal felt extremely guilty about having not re-paid the two pounds to the psychiatrist but not the least guilty about having bashed the old lady. The guilt had been displaced. One can imagine that man telling a psychotherapist how guilty he was about not having re-paid the two pounds, but not mentioning at all the old lady whom he had bashed. In such a situation, it is common for the psychotherapist to miss the displacement. Where there is neurotic guilt or psychotic guilt, there is also real guilt that cannot be borne. Also, in such a case, conscience is stifled and replaced by a savage superego. I point this out so as to make clear the difference between healthy conscience and a savage superego. The persecuting jabs of a savage superego are not signals from *participated being* but signs that the latter is walled off and not accessible to the rest of the personality.

Now, having ascertained that the obliteration of *participated being* is the source of all mental disturbance, it is clear that the establishment of *participated being* as the fountainhead of emotional life in the personality is the guarantor of mental health and sound emotional development. However, we realize with some wonder that this is also the source of religious life in mankind.

We often get into trouble when we start to discuss science, religion, and aesthetics because we concretize them into things. We *reify* them, to use a sociological term. Science, aesthetics, and religion refer to three different mental vertices. There is a mental attitude that is scientific, a mental attitude that is aesthetic, and a mental attitude that is religious. Let us understand first the attitude that is scientific.

If I plan to make a table to fit into a corner of my sitting-room, I do not just start hacking away at a piece of wood willy-nilly. I judge the size of table I want and its shape, and then I start to take measurements for its height, the measurements for its width and depth, measure the thickness of the top and then that of the legs, and so on. All these calculations can be set out on paper before a saw has touched a plank of wood. My purpose in this endeavour is to make something for my use. When I make the measurements and calculations, I am being scientific. It is the attitude of mind that I have to adopt when I want to adapt the natural environment to my use. The process necessary for the adaptation of the environment for the use of man is the scientific attitude. There was no science before humanization (except to a minimal extent in the tool-making activities of chimpanzees and gorillas), because other animals adapted themselves to the environment. But man has the power to adapt the environment to himself. As soon as he turns his mind to this end, he is in the scientific domain.

When I decide to shape the legs of my table in a tapering style, I do so because it pleases me. It has no direct practical use. I make it beautiful to please my soul. This is my only motivation for it. This is the aesthetic state of mind.

What, then, is the mental attitude that we call "religious"? Whereas in the scientific and aesthetic the environment is shaped to my desire, here something has a claim on me rather than the other way round. This something is what I have named *participated being*. Now, you will notice that there are two aspects to *participated being*: it is both me and not-me. Remember that motto of the Upanishads: THAT THOU ART. I am it and, at the same time, I am not it. This dual perspective upon *participated being* is essential to our understanding of religion. In the religious state of mind, I act according to the principle that *participated being* has a claim upon me.

Now I want to emphasize something. *Participated being* is NOT God or a deity of any kind. We are all so imbued with the godhead that has come to us through the Judaeo–Christian tradition that it is difficult for us to conceptualize the difference between this and *participated being*. In the realization of *participated being* we *are* IT, but with the deity we are not. Although in the Christian revelation God became man so that humanity could share God's life, this was initiated from an act by the Deity outside us. (The term "God" has been used to mean what I call *participated being*. For instance, Spinoza used it in this sense.) Once this idea of the deity is established, then our submission to it is capable of being antagonistic to *participated being*. In my book *Emotion and Spirit*, I differentiate between *primitive religion* and *mature religion*. *Primitive religion*, which erects a deity to which we bow our heads, is antagonistic to our mental health and emotional development. According to the Theravada Tradition, the Buddha was an atheist, and yet few would deny that the teaching and organization that he started is religious. In the West, we are so imbued with the Judaeo–Christian faith that it is difficult for us to conceptualize a religious tradition that is specifically atheist. We are THAT so the claim of THAT, of *participated being*, is the fullness of our being.

My wife, my children, my mother, my father, and all those I share my life with *are participated being*, so the claim of *participated being*, the voice of conscience, is the fulfilment of my nature and of theirs. The Upanishads' statement is: THAT YOU ARE (i.e. all of you). So this claim of *participated being* is a claim upon *me*. Now, paradoxically, the reification of "me-ness", is the deity and it interferes with the realization of *participated being*. I believe that Freud's critique of religion in *The Future of an Illusion* (1927c) is correct if religion is just what he believed it to be. His critique is of primitive religion, and, if this alone is being considered, then he is right to say, as he does, that it saps energy that is needed by the psyche for scientific enquiry. Freud, however, was ignorant of what I have referred to in my book as "mature religion". The difference between "mature" and "primitive" religion is made more difficult through semantic confusion because mystics within Judaism, Christianity, and Islam have referred to *participated being* as god, but as soon as one examines closely the reality to which they are referring, it is clear to see that it bears no relation to Yahweh, God, or Allah. The god of St John of the Cross bears no resemblance to the God whom people go to the synagogue, church, or mosque to worship. Aldous Huxley (1980) has shown, to me convincingly, that mystics in the three great Western religions—Judaism, Christianity, and Islam—and those within the tradition of Hinduism, Buddhism, or Taoism all share the same vision: THAT THOU ART.

You may be saying that this is at a far remove from the work of psychoanalysis in the consulting-room, yet the exact opposite is the case. I want to give you just one example. This man was in despair that his life was so discontinuous. He had moved jobs umpteen times, had been in and out of six marriages, and held no persevering conviction. "Shall I do this or shall I do that? To be or not to be?" There was no cohering centre, and his outer life was an expression of this inner state of affairs. He came for analysis because he wanted, he said, to be a person before he entered the grave. If I made an interpretation that made sense of an array of phenomena, I found that my mind would begin to wander in an aimless manner, and his subsequent speech was dissociated from something that was emotionally very meaningful and had a lullaby effect upon me. Something prevented me from remaining connected to meaningful cohesion. I realized that this something also prevented him from maintaining the cohesion that he so direly wanted. The transference is to be understood like this: *participated being* is not known directly, but its failure to be established as creative reality in the personality is experienced as chronic frustration. *Participated being* is crippled in its expression. What I experience as analyst is what is occurring within the patient's mind, and it tells me how *participated being* is being smothered. It may at first seem a paradox that the source of creative action lies in *participated being*. This is because that is the locus of what is most me within the personality and yet is not mine—in other words, it does not belong to me because it *is* me. I believe much confusion would be avoided if this were grasped. There are two poles within which modern humanity has taken refuge: that of self-surrender to a deity (which can be incarnate in an institution, ideology, or a person) in the service of which the personal is crushed, and that of surrender to self-expression which on the surface looks personal but also represents the crushing of the personal. This polarity can easily be observed in social groupings and also in the fluctuations in the psychic life of the individual.

* * *

Let me take stock of where we are. I have made two statements: that the establishment of *participated being* is the foundation stone of mental health and sound emotional development *and* that it is the core of religion.

I am talking here of "natural religion"—that is, religion whose foundation resides naturally in mankind and whose dictates are mediated through conscience. It is rational, as opposed to revealed religion which is not. The difference between natural religion and revealed religion needs to be understood. When I act according to the inner principles of natural religion, I act according to the principles of *participated being*—according to this being that is more me than me and yet it is THAT. When acting according to this principle of natural religion, I act creatively. When I am in accord with the THAT within me, when it is that which acts and which I allow to act, then I act creatively. The THAT is the creative principle within me. [Now, strange to say, this is how Groddeck (1923) conceptualized DAS ES—THE IT. Freud adopted this term of Groddeck's in the structural model but changed it into an instinctive force—the Id.] Narcissism—me-ness—smothers this creative principle within. The sense of creativity flowing from a non-me principle within is well known to artists and writers. Rudyard Kipling referred to the Daemon within him and says at one point that he could not write because the Daemon had left him. (Some will protest that many of the most creative people have been extraordinarily narcissistic. I would not deny it for a moment, but I would maintain that the creative in them does not flow from the narcissistic currents in their personality. The creative moments even in the most creative of people are often not numerous. There is frequently a tension between the creative and narcissistic that becomes the primordial struggle of their lives.) Being faithful to the principles of natural religion is a state of mind described by Melanie Klein as the depressive position.

In revealed religion, I bow my head to a deity and offer sacrifice to it in fear and trembling. The mental state associated with this is what Melanie Klein named the paranoid–schizoid position. Revealed religion, which is the sophisticated elaboration of primitive religion, is the cultural reification of this primitive state of mind. In this state, the *participated being* is obliterated. Revealed religion is the enemy of natural religion. This does not mean that all members of revealed religion are necessarily in this state. I have already instanced the mystics, who are those who have, through contemplation, internalized in a deep way the reality of natural religion. There is a constant tension within revealed religion between the primitive and the mature. There are many members of the revealed religions who have managed to escape the strictures of the deity and avoided being crushed, but the message of those is nearly always that it has been a severe struggle. I believe that Gerald Manley Hopkins has expressed himself in this sense.

In *Emotion and Spirit*, I have instanced Socrates as a religious teacher. Although he is looked upon by most (*pace* I. F. Stone) as a giant in the annals of ethical thinking, he has not been divinized as has been the case with the Buddha in the Mahayana Tradition, Jesus, and Mohammed. Socrates was the teacher of natural religion *par excellence*. He did not reach, as far as we can see, the depth of realization that was achieved by the seers of the Upanishads; although he translated his intellectual vision into the language of the market-place, it was also a vision that could be achieved through rational process. The impetus to moral action is the Good, and Socrates defends his position through painstaking logical argument. (The matter can also be argued through the concept of Justice, as Stuart Hampshire, 1989, has done.) We do not believe that it is possible to prove the existence of the Good, of *participated being*, through logical argument. It is the sort of reality that can only be proved through what Cardinal Newman called "the convergence of probabilities", which is similar to the "selected fact", a term proposed by Poincaré and more latterly adopted by Wilfred Bion. If I stand up and say that I do not see why I should not be sadistic, why I should not harden my heart against friendly gestures towards me, why I should not be bloody-minded if I want to be, why I should not despise blacks or treat women as sexual objects, there are no convincing arguments based on Darwinian principles against any of these positions or any such other. My interlocutor might say that if I proceed in such a direction I will make a muck of my life, but my answer is that it is my life and that I am entitled to make a muck of it if I want to. The devout reader of the Upanishads will try to show

me that my life is not my own, he will enunciate to me the principle of THAT THOU ART—and I will say, rubbish. This is the place
where the Socratic method falls down, because it assumes good-
will on my part. Each of the great religious movements that I
have outlined in my book—Judaism, Christianity, Islam, Zoroas-
trianism, Hinduism, Buddhism, and Socratic religion—have particular mental attitudes not shared by the others. It is my view
that in this era in which values have collapsed, we cannot afford
to cling to any one system but, rather, must search out the good
in each. The Upanishads has the primordial vision, but it does not
have an elaborated theory of moral action. Buddhism does have
such a theory, but it exists in a realm cut off from human intimacy and rational argument. Socrates does exist in the thrall of
mankind, but he lacks the profundity of vision enjoyed by the
Upanishads. Judaism, Christianity, and Islam have a vision of
compassion, but are all overshadowed by a deity that demands
sacrifice and worship. What we are looking for is a religion that
fits mature emotional action in the modern world.

* * *

In *Emotion and Spirit*, I have used the phrase "emotional action" to
describe an activity that is differentiated from motor action. I turn
to someone and say "I love you"; I turn to another person and say
"I hate you"; I turn to another and say "I envy you" and to another "I respect you". These statements describe my activities towards the other person. I think that you will agree that these
activities are very different—I love, I hate, I envy, I respect—and
yet I believe that we are all hard put to describe accurately the
inner activity of which these words are the description. It is the
job of psychoanalysis to make a scientific investigation of these
hidden activities. I am in close association with another person—
maybe my wife, my father, my mother, my children, my colleague at work—and I envy this other person or, alternatively, I
respect him or her. The difference between these two activities is
enormous. The other person, over time, will have two quite different experiences. I have, of course, chosen only four of these
activities, but they are numerous and cover a wide spectrum: I
suspect, I disdain, I scorn, I adore, I revere, I trust, and so on.

The social change, often associated with secularization, since the Industrial Revolution has witnessed a shift from extended family patterns to the nuclear family. This, you will understand, is shorthand for a change where personal emotional attitudes are the governing force in social engineering. In traditional society, I could despise my wife, and the social structure would hold the marriage in place. Today, it would lead to divorce. These hidden emotional activities, then, are what govern the patterns of living in the world today. This is certainly so in what is known as the Western world, but it is becoming so in many other societies also. It is in the sphere of these activities, then, that the core values of religion are most urgently required. What has happened, however, is that traditional religion has been rightly jettisoned because it cannot do the job that the patterns of modern living require it to do. There have been two general pathways that have resulted from this situation: either a moral decadence manifested in violence, drugs, suicide, depression, and existential despair, or a pathetic retreat into fundamentalist sects, astrology, fortune-telling, tarot cards, ufology, and an ever-widening panoply of secular superstition.

My thesis, then, is that the core values—or core value—of religion is necessary in our times, and that it needs to be mediated into the sphere of emotional activity as it occurs in the relations of intimacy between people. What I have referred to as primitive religion and revealed religion, its elaborated successor, have been ditched and natural religion put in its place.

What I am maintaining is that *participated being* is the foundation stone of values and that, if I am to answer the question that I posed at the beginning—"on what basis do I judge paranoia unfavourably?"—it is to be traced back to that solidity of which our being is woven: *participated being*. It is out of this that we make our judgement that paranoia is mentally deviant. In a similar, way we judge sadism and masochism to be deviant or mentally perverse.

Every interpretation contains a judgement. This is the religious axis within psychoanalysis. It is this axis that gives an interpretation its cogency, its power to penetrate beneath the surface. However, if psychoanalysis consisted in just this, it would be a secular form of preaching. Of course, it often is precisely this and has been criticized extensively for being an agent of social control within conventional society. This religious axis, therefore, easily degenerates into a series of ritualistic, well-worn interpretations that are ineffective. Psychoanalysis is also scientific, and that axis is equally essential if the process is to remain alive and potent. I would now like to examine this scientific axis.

Whereas the religious preacher always *knows* the object of his faith, the scientist does not. The scientist investigates his world; he is on a journey of discovery. To every answer that is arrived at, there is another "why?". Each answer is another point on that chart to answer the big question: How does the mind function? The answer to this question has a use. It is of direct use to the patient, but its use is wider than this. It stands as a hypothesis for further investigation. I will give an example of this. A man was in distress, and I offered him an extra session. He was initially grateful and felt cared for. Then he had another thought: "He has offered me this session because he wants the money." He had an inhibition about voicing this second thought, and the scientist in me asked the question (of myself)—"Why is there an inhibition about expressing this thought?" The next day he asked for a change of time. It emerged that this had not been requested for any practical reason but to discover whether I was full of free times, which would confirm the thought about the expression of which there had been an inhibition. With further investigation, it became clear that the inhibition screened not a thought but a delusional conviction. This led to a hypothesis that inhibition is a mechanism to screen delusion—a hypothesis that could be tested to see whether it applied in the wider social context. Also, if this were the case and a patient in analysis becomes less inhibited, does this represent a transformation of delusion into thought? And if this is the case, how does this occur? This leads to further scientific investigation. As points on the chart become established, it then becomes possible to generate a theory to make sense of these new observations.

Each interpretation—each new judgement—is also the establishment of a psychological fact. The religious axis and the scientific axis intersect. Three factors need to be investigated, then, in analysis: the religious, the scientific, and the intersection of these two. The religious and scientific axes are necessary to establish a psychological fact. In the emotional sphere, psychological facts are established by judgement and by the human thrust to know, or curiosity. In an unpublished paper, "The Nature of Reality", presented a few years ago in Melbourne, I established, I hope, that reality is the product of a value judgement. That paper needs to be put next to this chapter in order that it receives its proper balance from the scientific axis *and* the intersection of the two.

It is these three factors that establish the identity of psychoanalysis. It is possible by using these criteria to distinguish between psychoanalysis and that which is not. If it is religion without the scientific axis, it degenerates into primitive religion; if it is scientific without being religious, there is theory detached from emotional reality. In other words, without these three factors the progress engaged in is neither scientific nor religious but aesthetic. It may be very beautiful and I may be filled with good feelings, but there is no substance, no knowledge of myself. What I am in possession of is an illusion. This latter condition is the state of affairs in much psychoanalytic practice and in most psychotherapy. It is the reason for my statement at the beginning that there is to-day a *malaise* in the psychoanalytic and psychotherapeutic movement. There is, I believe, the genuine article. In this chapter I have tried to establish those criteria through which it is possible to distinguish the genuine from the fake.

CHAPTER TWELVE

A religious man
who doesn't believe in God

Samuel M. Stein

> *And I know that the hand of God is the promise of my own*
> *And I know that the spirit of God is the brother of my own*
>
> Walt Whitman, *Song of Myself,* 1881

When I originally embarked on what has now developed into a provocative and thought-provoking project, I had no intention of adding a final chapter. However, it seemed somehow important to describe the impact of the essays I had collected together, and how my own understanding of both psychoanalysis and religion had changed over time. I therefore set myself the task of trying to describe the evolution of my current beliefs based on the explorations inherent in editing a work of this nature and striving to understand one's own internal world.

In early 1994, about the time when I first approached the contributors, I also embarked on a period of private study to enhance my psychoanalytic understanding. The work of Wilfred Bion had presented itself as an enigmatic and seldom-taught approach, and

I decided to spend some time trying to understand his theoretical and clinical paradigms. What emerged behind his attempts to render psychoanalysis more scientific was an extremely religious man whose theories were an attempt to understand both religion and spirituality based on his experiences in two world wars. His work looked towards the dark and formless infinite of human awareness, represented as spirituality and the experience of ultimate truth. Bion described these experiences as at-one-ment or O, in contrast to the representation of knowledge which he called K. I found a gradual merging taking place between my past experiences and religious practice, the reading and understanding of Bion's work, the task of editing *Beyond Belief* and my own growing sense of spirituality.

I was born and grew up in Johannesburg, South Africa, as part of a comfortingly tight-knit but proportionally insular Jewish community. My background was what I would call traditional orthodox. It was neither the black-hatted and earlocked life of the ultra-orthodox, nor the more liberal life of the Jewish reform movement. I enjoyed growing up within this community as everything was stable, secure and readily explicable. As a result, I experienced little reason or desire to question any of the traditions and beliefs that determined my day-to-day life. The superstition and mysticism that were mixed in with the more formal aspects of the religion served only to add mystery and excitement. This comforting insularity was easily maintained in a country already divided along racial lines.

My interest in psychoanalysis and psychotherapy evolved over a period of ten or fifteen years. It began with participation in multi-racial youth groups and extended into therapeutic communities and crisis-intervention work. I was able to expand these ideas and experiences still further when I arrived in Oxford to undertake my basic training in psychiatry. In psychoanalysis, I found a clinical and theoretical paradigm that seemed to fit neatly with my own personality, intellectual interest and emotional capacity. As with many people who find a new and ego-syntonic way of understanding life and the world around them, I became actively wedded to the precepts of analytic thought. I was willing to accept the accumulated wisdom of analysts past and present on faith, without questioning too closely the underpinning rationale behind these practices.

However, I found myself increasingly questioning my religious beliefs and slowly came to realize that much of my religious observance was done by rote or to allay anxiety, without any real in-depth understanding. I therefore decided to study Judaica in an attempt to manage better my increasing disquiet. I learned of the Kabbalah or mystical doctrines of Judaism, of the pseudo-messianic figures and of the *sitra achra* which represents the demonic "other side" of the divine universe. Yet, even after two years of study, this course of action only served to enhance my sense of uncertainty, and over time it became increasingly difficult to maintain a simultaneous belief in both religion and psychoanalysis. I thought that either one paradigm or the other would have to give way. This led to intense internal struggles, as Judaism had been the foundation on which my life had been built and I now stood to lose these long-cherished views in favour of an exciting exploration of the human psyche. The more I learned about psychoanalysis, the more the cornerstones of my existence were brought into question.

Resolving this dilemma would have been relatively straightforward if I could simply have transferred my allegiance in a rational and cognitive manner from Judaism to psychoanalysis. Unfortunately, the religious force is very powerful within man, often operating at an unconscious or even archetypal level. In essence, it represents a social component of instinctual functioning and has its origins in the inherent human desire to discover the meaning of life, to understand the truth of our existence and to grasp the reality of death. It is therefore hardly surprising that our primitive roots lead inevitably towards the belief in a universal spirit as protection against uncertainty and the fear of being alone. The concept of God or the Devil is then introduced to substantiate acts of faith, and rituals are developed in an attempt to control the spirit world by highly elaborate ceremonies including prayer and invocation. Whether the religious force is located in God, in the people, or in the priesthood, the decisions that result always carry unquestionable certainty. Therefore, whilst religious fashions may change, the fundamental nature of religion itself does not alter, as there is a shared and vested interest within a community in maintaining an existent cosmology.

These developments are reflected in two of Bion's key contributions to psychoanalytic thinking—maternal reverie and the concept of container and contained. The "contained" evacuates unpleasure in order to get rid of it, whilst the "container" accepts and modifies these primitive emotions and transforms them into a coherent and meaningful pattern. In maternal reverie, the infant's own feelings are similarly too powerful to be contained within his personality and he therefore arouses in his mother feelings of which he wishes to be rid. She accepts these unwanted feelings and modifies them so that they can be taken back by the infant in a more tolerable form. This shared activity determines the infant's later capacity for thought, as the product of container–contained is meaning, and the relationship between mother and infant provides the basis for learning from experience. A mother's capacity to be totally preoccupied by her infant is thus expressed by reverie, and, if children are loved by their mother in this way, they will develop the capacity to think and the means by which to gain some control of their internal and external world. Mental health is therefore based on the responses of the parents to the needs of the infant—their capacity to intuitively contain the unthinkable, unknowable and indescribable experiences of the infant and survive.

This intimate relationship with the mother, and the related experiences of reverie and containment, can been seen as the prototype for later intense emotional interactions, which Bion called O. They are individual and highly personal experiences that he described as ultimate reality, absolute truth, the infinite or the thing-in-itself. O may also represent "darkness" and "formlessness", as well as unknowable aspects of psychic reality. According to Bion, there is a primitive and fundamental psychic need to know this absolute or ultimate truth whose presence can be recognized and felt, although it can only be described as an aspiration within the human mind. Verbal, musical and artistic modes of communication are all transformations of O as they are attempts to achieve contact with psychic reality and allow the indefinable characteristics of O to evolve into conscious thought. Scientists, painters, musicians and artists are therefore all attempting to search for and display some aspect of this truth. It is essential for healthy mental growth, which depends on truth and without which the personality deteriorates. O is thus a state of "becoming"—a feeling of oneness with the world, a feeling of being one with the whole and a feeling of connectedness with others.

For Bion, the transformation involved in "becoming" or O was inseparable from the feeling of "becoming one with God" because the experience of at-one-ment with God resembled the sensuous fulfilment and harmonious mental growth inherent in successful reverie. By containing uncertainty, loneliness and unthinkable experiences, the mother–infant relationship thus serves as a potential prototype for the later belief in God, and the quality of our parenting will therefore determine whether God can be "good-enough". Given the infant's initial defencelessness and neediness, it seems inevitable that the human model of God will readily come to reflect an ultimately benign but very powerful parent now idealized as a religious god or goddess. However, the roles of mothers and fathers in relation to their infant's well-being are very different. Winnicott (1964) suggested that it was the father's role to protect the mother–infant dyad by turning outwards to deal with their surroundings. He provides a space in which the mother can turn inwards to the circle created by her arms at the centre of which is the baby. In contrast to this maternal provision of O, the father's relationship with the child can instead be seen as the prototype for what Bion called K as he, the father, provides an important link with the outside world, including reality and knowledge. In this sense, the evolution of organized religion may be more akin to paternally generated processes of "knowing" or K, as it may represent an attempt to explain the formless, infinite and often ineffable experiences which mirror those of infancy and childhood. Seeking God can therefore be seen as an attempt to restore the containing reverie of the mother or the external protection of a paternalistic figure. It may be that those who seek to re-create a sense of maternal holding look for spiritual experiences, whilst those who seek paternal protection look more actively towards organized religion.

It is important to differentiate between these mystical and religious experiences, as transcendent moments of spirituality are not automatically equatable with religious undertakings. The basic human dimensions of spirituality (O) derive from instinctual archetypal roots and should not be given religious overtones as if they prove the factual existence (K) of God. This results, as has happened in so many religions, in an anthropomorphic model of God in which a dead or imagined object is animated and endowed with human attributes in order to be worshipped in a very structured and ritualized manner. These objects are chosen specifically because they are dead or imaginary, as thoughts or feelings attributed to them cannot be either proved or disproved. By localizing individual or social thoughts and feelings in a God who confers an authoritative sense of the truth, the human craving for validation is satisfied. Personal desires are externalized and handed over to the notion of God, yielding meaning and answers that are then viewed as God-given. In this sense, God is an externalization of the internal object world, but His concrete embodiment allows absolute values to be deemed so "in the eyes of God". These concrete representations are in direct contrast with Freud's description of the truth of religious doctrines as dependent on inner experience.

Bion's conception of O similarly relies on individual relationships with internal representations of loved persons, which may come to reflect an inner sense of God. Instead of seeking definitive answers through organized religion, these numinous events represent a capacity for tolerating uncertainty without rushing to premature conclusions, allowing the state of incoherence and incomprehensibility to endure until a new coherence emerges. This emerging coherence may be experienced as a sense of awe and inspiration, leading to feelings of bliss, wonder and ecstasy reminiscent of early contact with a caring mother and the development of a capacity to think. Mystics and men of genius have appeared in all religions, at all times and in all places with the capacity to describe this power or force of being in direct contact with the sense of O/God/mother. According to Bion, it is not possible for the ordinary member of a community to make direct contact with or be at one with O/God/mother, and it is therefore a function of society to make the mystical ideas available to ordinary members of the group. Laws in society, dogma in religion, and rules in mathematics and science, which can all be represented by K, act for the benefit of those who are not by nature able to have a direct experience of O.

My own journey away from religion and towards spirituality began as a young student. As prescribed religious practice became more limiting and frustrating, I tried instead to expand my awareness through life experiences, reading, travelling and meeting new people. I heard for the first time of Meister Eckhart, Ruysbroek and St John of the Cross, and I was increasingly able to empathize with writers and travellers who spoke of the ultimate reality of things, the blessedness of union with God, the flight from the Alone to the At-one and the Dark Night of the Soul. I also heard and read about the Absolute being Infinite, of the Absolute as Reality, of attaining reality by knowledge and of being, for a moment in time, at one with the Absolute. Others described how the Absolute is nowhere and everywhere, that it transcended permanence and change, whole and part, finite and infinite. Its completeness and perfection were unrelated to time; it was truth and freedom. Whilst worldly travel was inherently appealing, it slowly dawned on me that the journey that I needed to undertake was not geographical but, rather, a psychological exploration of myself. I therefore engaged more and more actively in psychoanalytic theory and practice, as I felt that it reflected many of these intangible spiritual ideas through concepts such as fusion, part-objects, space, time and truth.

As with my earlier experiences of religion, my initial attempts to understand psychoanalysis were very much a quest for knowledge. However, what I emerged with from these explorations was a growing sense of who I was and the validity of what I could feel. It was a fundamentally indescribable experience and yet one with which innumerable people are aware. In its truest sense, it was a quest for O, and, as this awareness expanded, structures of any sort became less important and even limiting. This core sense of "being" is the soul of both religious discourse and psychoanalysis. But, within both paradigms, it is also a fearful prospect to perceive of or relate to the invisible and unthinkable nature of at-one-ment or unity with O. Practitioners within psychoanalysis and religion, especially those who relate more easily to K, may therefore conspire with equal intensity to create rituals, structures and a sense of certainty as unknown ideas are frightening and thus hated.

Being ignorant and tolerating doubt is also unpleasant, and human beings have an investment in knowing "the answer". When confronted with the unknown, individuals and societies are pressured from within to closure the discussion and fill the free space or void by giving boundaries to the infinite. Defences are instituted to put a stop to disagreeable feelings of ignorance, and there is a tendency to escape back into what is already known. But knowledge (K) is capable only of yielding information about something; it is not a state of "being", and it often represents the temptation to terminate prematurely a stage of uncertainty. This sense of "knowing" is used to avoid "becoming" or "being"—K as opposed to O. Religion and psychoanalysis, if not able to embrace uncertainty, will simply come to represent (in common with many scientific developmental processes) a progression from the open "void and formless infinite" of Bion to "saturated" formulations that are finite and closed: for example, the transition from the dark and formless Godhead of Meister Eckhart to the "knowable" trinity which is apprehensible by man; or from the far-reaching hypotheses of psychic life on which psychoanalysis is founded to the structured and formalized application of many psychotherapies.

What has become apparent to me is that spirituality and psychotherapy are extremely congruent as both serve to give life meaning. Both approaches facilitate deep personal disclosure, and both hold to produce change for the better. Psychoanalysis may even produce something close to religious conversion. The patient's presentation will therefore be significant in representing his view of O, and the therapist should try to achieve a frame of mind in which he is receptive to the O of the analytic experience, especially those evolved elements such as dreams and myths. Psychoanalytic discovery, like spirituality, requires a transformation from K to O—a move from "knowing" to "being". The value of both religious and psychoanalytic interventions will be therapeutically greater if they are conducive to transformations in O.

I have now emerged from a religious background and a sustained period of analysis to the realization that both were journeys of equal value and intensity. Neither psychotherapy nor religion proved inherently superior, nor did the belief in one in-validate or balance out a belief in the other. Instead, both are part of the same wider picture that will accompany me from the cra-dle to the grave. I have also come to accept that psychoanalysis cannot answer my questions on religion, and it cannot add to or speak against the validity of religious phenomena. My move from religion to psychoanalysis was not the simplistic scale that I ini-tially visualized, with one side waxing as the other waned. It could be better represented as part of a continuum of develop-ment, progressing from religion through psychoanalysis to spir-ituality.

What came to matter most was monitoring my own internal world, with greater emphasis placed on feelings of honesty and personal truth. This quest for personal truth ultimately tran-scended both psychoanalysis and religion, and my original belief in both began to decline. What was "known" no longer mat-tered—only what seemed to be true within myself, within others and within my relationships with them retained any validity. As a result, I have found myself increasingly questioning both clergy-men and psychoanalysts who insist that there is only one accept-able way in which beliefs can be expressed or put into practice. I have also come to realize that much of what I learned about and accepted without question in both religion and psychoanalysis was "saturated", to use Bion's term, by those who perpetuated traditions based on anxiety, resistance to change, blind trust and faith. If anything, their approach was defined by closed and rigid beta-element thinking that prevented individual and personal de-velopment from K to O. I can therefore no longer believe in either religion or psychoanalysis as securely or comfortably as I had pre-viously been able to achieve.

Instead of simply finding linear answers to the questions that initially motivated me, developing an insight into the work of Wilfred Bion and bringing *Beyond Belief* to print has proved a re-markable journey in its own right. My journey from orthodox Judaism via psychoanalysis has now emerged as an undefined spirituality—a quest for oneness and personal truth. However, questioning some of what I believe and rejecting some of the pre-cepts on which Judaism is based does not equate with a rejection of my identity or pride in being Jewish. It is the cornerstone of my lifelong personal development and will always continue to be so. Equally, I will always value my personal experience of psychoanalysis, including the theoretical and clinical concepts that I have learned. Like Judaism in my personal life, psychoanalytic thinking will always stand as the cornerstone of my professional development and influence forever the way in which I work. However, having passed through both religion and psychoanalysis en route to where I am now, I have come to recognize that there is a place that extends beyond religion and beyond psychoanalysis too. In essence, therefore, I am a committed Freudian who has doubts about psychoanalysis, a proud Jew on the outskirts of Judaism, and a religious man who doesn't believe in God.

REFERENCES

Aberbach, D. (1989). Grief and mysticism. In: *Surviving Trauma* (pp. 83–109). New Haven, CT: Yale University Press.

Ahmad, Hazrat Mirza Tahir (1989). *Islamic terrorism? Murder in the Name of Allah*. Cambridge: Lutterworth Press.

Althusser, L. (1971). Freud and Lacan. In: *Lenin and Philosophy and Other Essays* (pp. 177–202). London: New Left Books.

Assagioli, R. (1975). *Psychosynthesis*. London: Tavistock.

Baker, J. A. (1970). *The Foolishness of God*. London: Darton, Longman & Todd.

Berkhof, H. (1986). *Christian Faith: An Introduction to the Study of the Faith*. Grand Rapids, MI: William Eerdmans.

Berlin, I. (1991). *The Crooked Timber of Humanity*. London: Fontana Press.

Bion, W. R. (1961). *Experiences in Groups and Other Papers*. London: Tavistock Publications. [Reprinted London: Routledge, 1994.]

Bion, W. R. (1962). A theory of thinking. In: *Second Thoughts* (pp. 110–119). London: Karnac Books.

Bion, W. R. (1967). *Second Thoughts*. London: Heinemann Medical. [Reprinted London: Karnac Books, 1993.]

189

Black, D. M. (1993). What sort of a thing is a religion? *International Journal of Psycho-Analysis, 74*: 613–625.

Black, D. M. (1996). Abiding values and the creative present. *British Journal of Psychotherapy, 12*: 314–321.

Bolen, J. S. (1992). *Ring of Power*. San Francisco, CA: HarperCollins.

Britton, R. (1995). Psychic reality and unconscious belief. *International Journal of Psycho-Analysis, 76*: 19–23.

Buber, M. (1967). *On Judaism*. New York: Schocken Books.

Buber, M. (1970). *I and Thou* (transl. by W. Kaufmann). Edinburgh: T. & T. Clark.

Campbell, J. B. (1989). *An Open Life: Joseph Campbell in Conversation with Michael Toms*, edited by J. M. Maher & D. Briggs. New York: Harper & Row.

Carman, J. B. (1994). *Majesty and Meekness: A Comparative Study of Contrast and Harmony in the Concept of God*. Grand Rapids, MI: William Eerdmans.

Casement, P. J. (1963). The paradox of unity. *Prism, 69*: 8–11.

Casement, P. J. (1964). "A false security?", *Prism, 88*: 28–30.

Casement, P. J. (1985). *On Learning from the Patient*. London: Tavistock Publications.

Casement, P. J. (1990). *Further Learning from the Patient*. London: Routledge.

Chapman, J. (1988). *Tell Me Who You Are*. Milton Keynes: Hanslope.

Chodorow, N. (1978). *The Reproduction of Mothering*. Berkeley, CA: University of California Press.

Chodorow, N. (1994). *Femininities, Masculinities, Sexualities: Freud and Beyond*. London: Free Association Books.

Cox, M. (1973). Dynamic psychotherapy and the Christian response: areas of congruence. *Christian, 1*: 1–12.

Cox, M. (1978a). *Structuring the Therapeutic Process: Compromise with Chaos*. London: Jessica Kingsley, 1995.

Cox, M. (1982). "I took a life because I needed one": psychotherapeutic possibilities with the schizophrenic offender-patient. *Psychotherapy and Psychosomatics, 37*: 96–105.

Cox, M. (1993). *The Group as Poetic Play-Ground: from Metaphor to Metamorphosis*. S. H. Foulkes Annual Lecture, 1990. London: Jessica Kingsley. (On cassette with readings from Shakespeare by Clare Higgins.)

Cox, M., & Grounds, A. (1991). The nearness of the offence: some theological reflections on forensic psychotherapy. *Theology* (March/April): 106–115.

Cox, M., & Theilgaard, A. (1987). *Mutative Metaphors in Psychotherapy: The Aeolian Mode.* London: Tavistock Publications/Routledge. (Reprinted London: Jessica Kingsley, 1997.)

Cox, M., & Theilgaard, A. (1994). *Shakespeare as Prompter: The Amending Imagination and the Therapeutic Process.* London: Jessica Kingsley.

Crapanzano, V. (1992). Talking (about) psychoanalysis. In: *Hermes' Dilemma & Hamlet's Desire: On the Epistemology of Interpretation* (pp. 142–143). Cambridge, MA: Harvard University Press.

Crook, J. (1990). Meditation and personal disclosure: the Western Zen retreat. In: J. Crook & D. Fontana (Ed.), *Space in Mind.* London: Element Books.

Crossan, J. D. (1988). *The Dark Interval: Towards a Theology of Story.* Sonoma, California: Polebridge Press.

Cullmann, O. (1951). *Christ and Time* (transl. by F. V. Filson). London: SCM Press.

Cupitt, D. (1997). *After God—The Future of Religion.* London: Weidenfeld & Nicolson.

da Vinci, L. (1952). *The Notebooks of Leonardo da Vinci,* edited by I. A. Richter (Ed.). Oxford: Oxford University Press.

Davies, P. (1992). *The Mind of God.* London: Penguin Books.

Dinnerstein, D. (1976). *The Mermaid and the Minotaur.* New York: Harper & Row.

Edelman, G. M. (1992). *Bright Air, Brilliant Fire.* New York: Basic Books.

Eliot, T. S. (1953). Tradition and the individual talent. In: *Selected Prose* (pp. 21–30). Harmondsworth: Penguin Books.

Estes, C. P. (1992). *Women Who Run with the Wolves.* London: Rider.

Fairbairn, W. R. D. (1944). Endopsychic structure considered in terms of object-relationships. In: *Psychoanalytic Studies of the Personality.* London: Tavistock, 1952.

Fordham, M. (1958). *The Objective Psyche.* London: Routledge & Kegan Paul.

Freud, A. (1966). *Normality and Pathology in Childhood: Assessments of Development.* London: Hogarth Press.

Freud, S. (1905d). *Three Essays on the Theory of Sexuality. S.E., 7.*

Freud, S. (1917e). Mourning and melancholia. *S.E., 14.*

Freud, S. (1927c). *The Future of an Illusion. S.E., 21.*

Freud, S. (1930a). *Civilization and its Discontents. S.E., 21.*

Friedman, M. (1982). *Martin Buber's Life and Work.* London/Tunbridge Wells: Search Press.

Fromm, E. (1960). *Psychoanalysis and Zen Buddhism*. London: Allen and Unwin.

Frosh, S. (1977). Fundamentalism, gender and family therapy. *Journal of Family Therapy, 19*: 417–430.

Fynn (1974). *Mr. God, This Is Anna*. London: Fountain.

Gallwey, P. (1990). The psychopathology of neurosis and offending. In: R. Bluglass & P. Bowden (Eds.), *Principles and Practice of Forensic Psychiatry* (chap. 4). London: Churchill Livingstone.

Gallwey, P. (1991). Social maladjustment. In: J. Holmes (Ed.), *Psychotherapy in Psychiatric Practice*. London: Churchill Livingstone.

Gallwey, P. (1996). Psychotic and borderline processes. In: C. Cordess & M. Cox (Eds.), *Forensic Psychotherapy*. London: Jessica Kingsley.

Gilkey, L. B. (1969). *Naming the Whirlwind: The Renewal of God-Language*. Indeanopolis, IN: Bobbs-Merril.

Gilkey, L. B. (1976). *Reaping the Whirlwind: A Christian Interpretation of History*. New York: Seabury Press.

Girard, R. (1987). *Things Hidden since the Foundation of the World* (transl. by S. Banns & M. Metteer). London: Athlone Press.

Goodison, L. (1990). *Moving Heaven and Earth*. London: Women's Press.

Gordon, R. (1993). *Bridges: Metaphor for Psychic Processes*. London Karnac Books.

Gorer, G. (1965). *Death, Grief and Mourning in Contemporary Britain*. London: Cresset.

Graham, W. A. (1987). *Beyond the Written Word: Oral Aspects of Scripture in the History of Religion*. Cambridge: Cambridge University Press.

Graves, R. (1961). *Collected Poems*. London: Cassell.

Groddeck, G. W. (1923). *The Book of the It*. New York: Vision Press.

Hampshire S. (1989). *Innocence and Experience*. London: Allen Lane/Penguin Press.

Hardy, A. (1979). *The Spiritual Nature of Man*. Oxford: Oxford University Press.

Hillier, W. (1959). *Granta*, 7 March.

Hopper, E. (1988). A brief clinical vignette. In: H. Cooper (Ed.), *Soul Searching: Studies in Judaism and Psychotherapy* (pp. 80–90). London: SCM Press.

Horwitz, R. (1988). *Buber's Way to I and Thou*. Philadelphia, PA: Jewish Publication Society.

Hubback, J. (1957). *Wives Who Went to College*. London: Heinemann.

Humphreys, A. R. (1968). Shakespeare's Histories and the "Emotion of Multitude". *Proceedings of the British Academy, 65*: 265–287.

Huxley, A. (1946). *Perennial Philosophy*. London: Chatto and Windus.

Huxley, J. (1964). *Essays of a Humanist*. Harmondsworth: Pelican/Penguin Books.

Issroff, J. (1983). A Reaction to Reading *Boundary and Space: An Introduction to the Work of D.W. Winnicott* by Madeleine Davis and David Wallbridge. *International Review of Psycho-Analysis*, 10: 231–235.

Issroff, J. (1993). "Reflections on *Yehovah*–God and other implications of Winnicott's concepts of the sense of continuity of being and of the 'female element' component of 'True Self'." Unpublished manuscript.

Jackson, M., & Williams, P. (1994). *Unimaginable Storms: A Search for Meaning in Psychosis*. London: Karnac Books.

James, W. (1902). *The Varieties of Religious Experience*. New York: Longmans, Green & Co. [Reprinted London: Penguin, 1985.)

Jeffries, R. (1883). *The Story of my Heart*. New York: Longmans, Green & Co. [Reprinted London: Penguin, 1938.]

Jones, J. W. (1991). *Contemporary Psychoanalysis and Religion: Transference and Transcendence*. New Haven, CT: Yale University Press.

Jung, C. G. (1958). *Psychology and Religion: West and East. Collected Works, 11.*

Jung, C. G. (1960). *Structure and Dynamics of the Psyche. Collected Works, 8.*

Jung, C. G. (1963). *Memories, Dreams, Reflections*. London: Collins/Routledge & Kegan Paul.

Jung, C. G. (1977). *The Symbolic Life. Collected Works, 18.*

Kierkegaard, S. (1843). *Fear and Trembling*. Princeton, NJ: Princeton University Press, 1941.

Klein, M. (1928). Early stages of the Oedipus conflict. In: *Love, Guilt and Reparation* (pp. 186–198). London: Hogarth, 1975. [Reprinted London: Karnac Books, 1992.]

Klein, M. (1946). Notes on some schizoid mechanisms. In: *Envy and Gratitude and Other Works* (pp. 1–24). London: Hogarth, 1975. [Reprinted London: Karnac Books, 1993.]

Klein, M. (1957). *Envy and Gratitude and Other Works 1946–1963*. London: Tavistock, 1975. [Reprinted London: Karnac Books, 1993.]

Klein, M. (1963). On the sense of loneliness. In: *Envy and Gratitude and Other Works 1946–1963* (pp. 300–313). London: Hogarth, 1975. [Reprinted London: Karnac Books, 1993.]

Kristeva, J. (1987). *In the Beginning Was Love: Psychoanalysis and Faith*. (transl. by A. Goldhammer). New York: Columbia University Press.

Kuhn, T. (1962). *The Structure of Scientific Revolutions*. Chicago, IL: University of Chicago Press.

Küng, H. (1981). *Does God Exist? An Answer for Today* (transl. by E. Quinn). New York: Random/Vintage Books.

Laing, R. D. (1967). *The Politics of Experience and The Bird of Paradise*. Harmondsworth: Penguin.

Laski, M. (1961). *Ecstasy: A Study of Some Secular and Religious Experiences*. London: Cresset Press.

Leibowitz, Y. (1989). *The Faith of Maimonides* (transl. by J. Glucker). Tel Aviv: MOD Press.

Maslow, A. H. (1970). *Religious Values and Peak Experiences*. London: Penguin, 1976.

Maxwell, M., & Tschedin, V. (1990). *Seeing the Invisible*. London: Arkana.

McGrath, P. J. (1995). Evil and the existence of God. In: *Believing in God*. Dublin: Wolfhound.

Meissner, W. W. (1984). *Psychoanalysis and Religious Experience*. New Haven, CT/London: Yale University Press.

Merton, R. K., Eco, U., & Donoghue, D. (1993). *On the Shoulders of Giants*. Chicago, IL: Chicago University Press.

Meissner, W. W. (1992). *Ignatius of Loyola: The Psychology of a Saint*. New Haven, CT: Yale University Press.

Mitchell, James (1967). *The God I Want*. London: Constable.

Mitchell, Juliet (1974). *Psychoanalysis and Feminism*. London: Penguin Books.

Ogden, C., & Richards, I. A. (1972). *The Meaning of Meaning* (10th ed.). London: Routledge & Kegan Paul.

Otto, R. (1923). *The Idea of the Holy* (transl. by J. W. Harvey). Oxford: Oxford University Press.

Panikkar, R. (1981). *The Unknown Christ of Hinduism*. London: Darton Longman and Todd.

Pascal, B. (1966). *Pensées* (transl. by A. J. Krailsheimer). London: Penguin Books.

Pontalis, J.-B. (1981). *Frontiers in Psychoanalysis: Between the Dream and Psychic Pain*. London: Hogarth Press.

Rey, H. (1977). The schizoid mode of being and the space–time continuum (beyond metaphor). *Journal of the Melanie Klein Society*, 4: 12–52.

Rilke, R. M. (1945). *Letters to a Young Poet*, Letter IV, 20 (transl. by R. Snell). Edinburgh: Edinburgh University Press.

Robinson, J. A. T. (1963). *Honest to God*. London: SCM Press.

Rose, J. (1993). *Why War?* Oxford: Blackwell.

Rubenstein, R. L. (1960). Psychoanalysis and the origins of Judaism. *Reconstructionist, 17*: 11–20.

Rubenstein, R. L. (1968). *The Religious Imagination*. Indianapolis, IN: Bobbs-Merrill.

Rubenstein, R. L. (1983). *The Age of Triage*. Boston: Beacon Press.

Rubenstein, R. L. (1992). *After Auschwitz: History, Theology, and Contemporary Judaism* (2nd revised ed.). Baltimore, MD: Johns Hopkins University Press.

Rubenstein, R. L., & Roth, J. K. (1986). *Approaches to Auschwitz*. Atlanta: John Knox Press.

Russell, B. (1919). *Introduction To Mathematical Philosophy* (chapter 14). London: Allen & Unwin.

Russell, B. (1930). Has religion made useful contributions to civilisation? In: *Why I Am Not a Christian*. London: Allen & Unwin, 1957.

Sayers, J. (1995). *The Man Who Never Was: Freudian Tales*. London: Chatto & Windus.

Shelley, P. B. (1811). The necessity of atheism. In: *Selected Prose Works of Shelley*. London: Watts & Co., 1915.

Shelley, P. B. (1821). Adonais: an Elegy on the death of John Keats. In: *An Anthology of English Verse*, edited by J. Drinkwater. New York: Houghton Mifflin.

States, B. O. (1978). *The Shape of Paradox: An Essay on waiting for Godot*. Berkeley, CA: University of California Press.

Storr, A. (1989). *Solitude*. London: Harper Collins.

Symington, J. (1985). The survival function of primitive omnipotence. *International Journal of Psycho-Analysis, 66*: 481–487.

Symington, N. (1994). *Emotion and Spirit*. London: Cassell. [Reprinted London: Karnac Books, 1998.]

Thich Nhat Hanh. (1995). *Living Buddha, Living Christ*. London: Rider.

Tillich, P. (1951). *Systematic Theology, Vol. 3*. Chicago, IL: University of Chicago Press.

Tracy, D. (1981). *The Analytical Imagination: Christian Theology and the Culture of Pluralism*. London: SCM Press.

Vermes, P. (1988). *Buber*. London: Weidenfeld and Nicolson.

Wallace, E. R. (1991). Psychoanalytic perspectives on religion. *International Review of Psycho-Analysis, 18*: 265–278.

Ward, G. (1996). *Theology and Contemporary Critical Theory*. London: Macmillan Press.

Weisman, A. D. (1972). *On Dying and Denying: A Psychiatric Study of Terminality*. New York: Behavioural Publications.

Wells, H. G. (1920). *The Outline of History*. London: Cassel.

Whale, J. S. (1967). *What Has Athens to Do with Jerusalem?* London: Epworth Press.

Wilber, K. (Ed.) (1984). *Quantum Questions*. Boston: Shambhala Publications.

Williams, Rev. H. A. (1960). *God's Wisdom in Christ's Cross*. London: A. R. Mowbray.

Williams, R. (1979). *Christianity and the Ideal of Detachment*. Frank Lake Lecture, 1988. Oxford: Clinical Theology Association.

Wilson, C. (1956). *The Outsiders*. London: Gollanz.

Winnicott, D. W. (1951). Transitional objects and transitional phenomena. In: *Collected Papers: Through Paediatrics to Psychoanalysis* (pp. 229–242). London: Tavistock Publications.

Winnicott, D. W. (1953). Transitional objects and transitional phenomena. *International Journal of Psycho-Analysis*, 34: 89–97.

Winnicott, D. W. (1958). The capacity to be alone. In: *The Maturational Processes and The Facilitating Environment* (pp. 29–36). London: Hogarth Press, 1965.

Winnicott, D. W. (1960). Ego distortion in terms of True and False Self. In: *The Maturational Processes and the Facilitating Environment* (pp. 140–152). London: Hogarth Press.

Winnicott, D. W. (1964). *The Child, the Family and the Outside World*. London: Pelican Books. [Reprinted London: Penguin, 1991.]

Winnicott, D. W. (1965). *Maturational Processes and the Facilitating Environment*. London: Hogarth Press.

Winnicott, D. W. (1971a). Playing: creative activity and the search for the self. In: *Playing and Reality* (pp. 53–64). London: Tavistock Publications.

Winnicott, D. W. (1971b). *Playing and Reality*. London: Tavistock Publications.

Winnicott, D. W. (1989). *Psycho-Analytic Explorations* (edited by C. Winnicott, R. Shepherd, & M. E. V. Davis). Cambridge, MA: Harvard University Press.

Winnicott, D. W. (1996). The Niffle. In: *Thinking About Children* (pp. 104–109), edited by R. Shepherd, J. Johns, & H. T. Robinson. London: Karnac Books.

Wisdom, J. (1944). Gods. In: *Philosophy and Psycho-Analysis* (pp. 149–168). Oxford: Blackwell, 1964.

Wisdom, J. (1950). Metaphysics. In: *Other Minds* (pp. 245–265). Oxford: Blackwell, 1965.

Wulff, D. M. (1997). *Psychology of Religion*. New York: Wiley.

INDEX

197

Mussolini, B., 87
mutative metaphor, 59
Myers, A., xvi
Myers, F., xv
mysticism, 106–107

narcissism, primary, 127
natural religion, 173, 174, 176
Newman, J. H., 174
Nietzsche, F., 9, 115
non-differentiation, primary, 103

O, Bion's concept of, 180–187
object:
    internal, 7, 8, 10, 184
    -relating, vs. use of object, 109
    -relations school, 64
    -relations theory, 98
    transitional, 107
        God as, 108
        religion as, 150
oedipal complex, 92, 149
    archetypal, 98
Ogden, C., 134
omnipotence, 76, 89, 107, 109, 164–
        166
    fantasies of, 97, 110
"Otsogian" critical apparatus, 58
Otto, R., 86
Oxford Movement (Moral Re-
        armament), 32

Padmasambhava, 4
Panikkar, R., 4, 5, 16, 17
paranoia, 163, 164, 176
    and survival instinct, 163
paranoid–schizoid position, 173
Parkes, C. M., xiii, 132–145
participated being, 169–177
Pascal, B., 6–10, 12, 14
paternalism, 75, 76
patriarchalism, 150
Paul, St., 65
"peak experiences", 36

Pentonville, H.M. Prison, 48
personality fragmentation, 111
Peruvian Psychoanalytic Society,
        118, 124
phatic language, 53
Plato, 11
poiesis, 42, 60–61
Poincaré, R. N. L., 174
polarities, 54–55
    congruous, 55–56
    incongruous, 57
Pond, D., 48
Pontalis, J.-B., 103, 106, 114
Popper, K., 68, 77
potential space, of transitional
        phenomena, 111, 114
Pound, E., 127
primary narcissism, 127
primitive religion, 171, 173, 176,
        178
projection, 21, 27, 89, 95, 97, 108,
        110, 117
    God as, 108
projective identification, 66, 108,
        128, 151
psychic health and religion, 15
psychic reality, 7, 100, 159, 182
psychoanalysis:
    evolution of, 4
    as religion, 62–81
psychosynthesis, 67, 68, 76

Quakerism, 17, 31, 32, 35, 37

Ramakrishna, 16
Rationalism, 34
Raven, C., 58, 59
reality, psychic, 7, 100, 159, 182
reflexivity, of body, 103
reincarnation, 99, 160
Religious Experience Research
        Centre, 36
"Resurrection Principle", 23–26
revealed religion, 173, 174, 176